THE
PSYCHOLOGY
OF
LOVE

Dr. Maxwell Shimba

Printed in the United States of America

SHIMBA
PUBLISHING

TABLE OF CONTENTS

INTRODUCTION

Love is a complex and multifaceted emotion that has been the subject of philosophical discourse, artistic expression, and scientific inquiry for centuries. From the ancient Greeks, who differentiated between eros (romantic love), philia (friendship), and agape (unconditional love), to contemporary psychologists who analyze its impact on human behavior and relationships, love continues to captivate and challenge our understanding.

The Ancient Greek Perspectives on Love

The ancient Greeks provided one of the earliest comprehensive explorations of love. They categorized love into several distinct types, each representing different aspects of the human experience. These classifications provide a useful framework for understanding the various dimensions of love.

1. Eros (Romantic Love): Eros is passionate, intense, and often driven by physical attraction and desire. It is the type of love that typically initiates romantic relationships, characterized by excitement and emotional intensity. The Greeks saw eros as a powerful and potentially dangerous force that could lead to irrational behavior.

2. Philia (Friendship): Philia represents deep friendship and companionship. It is the love between friends who share common values, mutual respect, and a strong bond. Unlike eros, philia is not based on physical attraction but on a sense of loyalty and shared experiences.

3. Agape (Unconditional Love): Agape is selfless, unconditional love that extends beyond personal interests. It is often associated with spiritual or altruistic love, where one cares for others without expecting anything in return. Agape is considered the highest form of love, exemplified by acts of compassion and kindness.

4. Storge (Familial Love): Storge refers to the love and affection found in family relationships, particularly between parents and children. It is a natural, instinctual love that grows out of familiarity and dependency.

5. Ludus (Playful Love): Ludus is playful and flirtatious love, often seen in the early stages of a relationship. It involves teasing, laughter, and fun, focusing on the enjoyment of the moment rather than long-term commitment.

6. Pragma (Practical Love): Pragma is practical, enduring love based on reason, duty, and long-term interests. It is the type of love that develops in long-term relationships,

where partners work together to achieve common goals and support each other through life's challenges.

Contemporary Psychological Perspectives on Love

Modern psychology has expanded on these ancient ideas, offering new insights into the nature of love and its role in human life. Psychologists have developed various theories to explain how love forms, how it evolves, and how it impacts our mental and emotional well-being.

1. Sternberg's Triangular Theory of Love: Psychologist Robert Sternberg proposed that love consists of three components: intimacy, passion, and commitment. Intimacy involves feelings of closeness and connectedness, passion refers to physical attraction and romantic desire, and commitment is the decision to maintain a long-term relationship. Different combinations of these components result in different types of love, such as romantic love (intimacy and passion), companionate love (intimacy and commitment), and consummate love (all three components).

2. Attachment Theory: Originally developed by John Bowlby and later expanded by Mary Ainsworth, attachment theory explores how early relationships with caregivers shape our ability to form and maintain love relationships in adulthood. Secure attachment, characterized by trust and a sense of safety, tends to result in healthier relationships, while

insecure attachment (anxious or avoidant) can lead to difficulties in love and intimacy.

3. The Five Love Languages: Dr. Gary Chapman proposed that people express and receive love in five distinct ways: words of affirmation, acts of service, receiving gifts, quality time, and physical touch. Understanding one's own love language and that of a partner can enhance communication and strengthen relationships.

Love in Art and Literature

Art and literature have long been mediums through which humans explore and express the complexities of love. From Shakespeare's timeless tales of romance and tragedy to modern cinema's portrayal of love in all its forms, artistic expressions of love reflect the diversity of human experience.

1. Literary Love: Classic literature offers a rich tapestry of love stories that explore the highs and lows of romantic relationships. For example, in "Pride and Prejudice" by Jane Austen, the evolving relationship between Elizabeth Bennet and Mr. Darcy highlights themes of personal growth, misunderstanding, and mutual respect.

2. Love in Art: Visual art has captured the essence of love through various styles and periods. Renaissance paintings often depicted romantic and divine love with an emphasis on

beauty and idealism, while modern art might explore the abstract and emotional aspects of love.

3. Love in Music: Music is a powerful vehicle for expressing love's emotions, from the joy and excitement of new love to the pain and longing of unrequited love. Love songs across genres resonate with listeners by tapping into universal feelings of connection and yearning.

The Science of Love

Advances in neuroscience and psychology have provided new insights into the biological and psychological mechanisms underlying love. Researchers have identified specific hormones and neurotransmitters that play critical roles in the experience of love.

1. Oxytocin and Vasopressin: Often referred to as the "love hormones," oxytocin and vasopressin are associated with bonding and attachment. Oxytocin is released during physical touch and intimacy, promoting feelings of closeness and trust. Vasopressin is linked to long-term commitment and partner bonding.

2. Dopamine: This neurotransmitter is associated with the brain's reward system and plays a key role in the pleasure and excitement of romantic love. The surge of dopamine experienced during the early stages of a romantic relationship can create feelings of euphoria and obsession.

3. Serotonin: Levels of serotonin, a neurotransmitter that regulates mood, can be affected by love. Early stages of romantic love are often characterized by lower levels of serotonin, which may contribute to obsessive thinking about a partner.

The Impact of Love on Human Behavior

Love profoundly influences human behavior, shaping our decisions, actions, and interactions. It can motivate selfless acts of kindness, inspire creativity and innovation, and foster deep personal connections.

1. Motivation and Goal-Setting: Love can drive individuals to achieve personal and professional goals. The desire to support and provide for loved ones can be a powerful motivator.

2. Behavioral Changes: Being in love often leads to changes in behavior, such as prioritizing a partner's needs, compromising on personal preferences, and investing time and effort into the relationship.

3. Health and Well-Being: Love has significant implications for physical and mental health. Positive, supportive relationships are associated with reduced stress, improved immune function, and greater overall happiness. Conversely, troubled relationships can contribute to mental health issues such as anxiety and depression.

The Challenges of Defining Love

Despite centuries of exploration and analysis, defining love remains a challenging task. Love is not a single emotion but a complex interplay of feelings, thoughts, and behaviors. It encompasses a wide range of experiences, from the passionate intensity of romantic love to the steady, enduring nature of long-term companionship.

1. Subjectivity: Love is deeply personal and subjective, meaning it can be experienced and expressed differently by each individual. Cultural, social, and personal factors all influence how we understand and define love.

2. Variability: Love can change over time, evolving through different stages and forms. What begins as a passionate romance may develop into deep friendship and partnership.

3. Multiplicity: Individuals can experience multiple types of love simultaneously, such as romantic love for a partner, familial love for children and parents, and altruistic love for humanity.

Love, in all its complexity and diversity, remains a fundamental aspect of the human experience. It shapes our relationships, influences our behavior, and contributes to our sense of meaning and fulfillment. By exploring the many dimensions of love—from its ancient philosophical roots to contemporary psychological theories—we can gain a deeper understanding of this powerful emotion and its impact on our lives.

As we embark on this journey through the psychology of love, we will delve into the biological, psychological, and cultural factors that shape our experience of love, offering insights and practical guidance for nurturing healthy, fulfilling relationships. Love is both a timeless and ever-evolving phenomenon, and by understanding its intricacies, we can enrich our own lives and the lives of those we love.

DR. MAXWELL SHIMBA

CHAPTER 01

DEFINING LOVE

Love is a complex and multifaceted emotion that has captivated humanity for centuries. It has been a central theme in philosophical discourse, artistic expression, and scientific inquiry. From the ancient Greeks, who differentiated between eros (romantic love), philia (friendship), and agape (unconditional love), to contemporary psychologists who analyze its impact on human behavior and relationships, love continues to captivate and challenge our understanding.

The Biological Basis of Love

Love has a profound impact on our brains and bodies. Understanding the biological mechanisms underlying love can provide insight into why it feels so powerful and can affect our behavior so deeply.

1. Hormones and Neurotransmitters:

- Oxytocin: Known as the "love hormone," oxytocin is released during physical touch, sexual activity, and childbirth. It promotes bonding, trust, and attachment.

- Dopamine: This neurotransmitter is associated with the brain's reward system and is linked to feelings of pleasure and euphoria experienced during the early stages of romantic love.

- Serotonin: Levels of serotonin can be affected by romantic love, often decreasing during the initial stages of infatuation, which can lead to obsessive thinking about a partner.

- Vasopressin: Similar to oxytocin, vasopressin is associated with long-term commitment and partner bonding.

2. Brain Activity:

- Limbic System: This area of the brain, which includes structures such as the amygdala and hippocampus, is involved in emotion processing and plays a significant role in the experience of love.

- Prefrontal Cortex: Responsible for decision-making and complex thought processes, the prefrontal cortex helps us evaluate and navigate our relationships.

Emotional and Cognitive Processes

Love is not just a biological response; it also involves complex emotional and cognitive processes. These processes help us form and maintain relationships, understand our feelings, and navigate the ups and downs of love.

1. Attachment Theory:

- Developed by John Bowlby and expanded by Mary Ainsworth, attachment theory explains how early relationships with caregivers shape our ability to form and maintain love relationships in adulthood. Secure attachment leads to healthier relationships, while insecure attachment (anxious or avoidant) can lead to difficulties in love and intimacy.

2. Sternberg's Triangular Theory of Love:

- Psychologist Robert Sternberg proposed that love consists of three components: intimacy, passion, and commitment. Different combinations of these components result in different types of love, such as romantic love (intimacy and passion), companionate love (intimacy and commitment), and consummate love (all three components).

3. Emotional Regulation:

- Love often involves intense emotions, and our ability to regulate these emotions can impact the quality of our relationships. Effective emotional regulation strategies, such as mindfulness and communication skills, can enhance relationship satisfaction and stability.

Types of Love

Love manifests in various forms, each with its own unique characteristics and significance. Understanding these different types of love can help us appreciate the diverse ways in which love enriches our lives.

1. Romantic Love:

- Romantic love combines passion, intimacy, and commitment. It often begins with intense attraction and infatuation and can evolve into a deep, enduring partnership. Romantic love is characterized by physical attraction, emotional connection, and a desire for long-term commitment.

2. Parental Love:

- Parental love is characterized by unconditional care and concern for one's children. It involves a deep sense of responsibility and a willingness to make sacrifices for the well-being of one's offspring. Parental love is crucial for the healthy development of children and provides a foundation for secure attachment.

3. Friendship (Philia):

- Friendship involves mutual respect, affection, and companionship. Unlike romantic love, it is not based on physical attraction but on shared experiences, values, and interests. Friendships provide emotional support, reduce stress, and contribute to overall well-being.

4. Self-Love:

- Self-love involves accepting and valuing oneself. It is not narcissistic but rather a healthy sense of self-worth and self-respect. Self-love is essential for mental health and well-being and influences how we engage in relationships with others.

5. Altruistic Love (Agape):

- Agape is selfless, unconditional love that extends beyond personal interests. It is often associated with acts of kindness, compassion, and service to others. Altruistic love promotes social cohesion and can enhance personal fulfillment and happiness.

Love and Mental Health

Love has significant implications for mental health and well-being. Positive, supportive relationships can enhance our emotional health, while troubled relationships can contribute to mental health issues.

1. Positive Impact on Mental Health:

- Love and supportive relationships are associated with reduced stress, lower rates of depression and anxiety, and greater overall happiness. Positive relationships provide emotional support, promote resilience, and improve self-esteem.

2. Challenges and Mental Health Issues:

- Troubled relationships can lead to mental health issues such as anxiety, depression, and low self-esteem.

Relationship conflicts, breakups, and unrequited love can cause significant emotional distress.

3. Therapeutic Interventions:

- Various therapeutic approaches can help individuals and couples navigate relationship challenges and improve their mental health. These include couple's therapy, individual therapy, and self-help strategies such as improving communication skills and developing emotional regulation techniques.

Love is a powerful and multifaceted emotion that plays a central role in human life. It encompasses a wide range of experiences, from the passionate intensity of romantic love to the steady, enduring nature of parental and friendship love. By exploring love from a psychological perspective, we can gain a deeper understanding of the biological, emotional, and cognitive processes that underlie this complex emotion.

As we continue our exploration in the subsequent chapters, we will delve deeper into the different types of love, their impact on our mental health and well-being, and practical strategies for nurturing healthy, fulfilling relationships. Understanding the psychology of love can enrich our own lives and help us build stronger, more meaningful connections with others.

CHAPTER 02

THE BIOLOGICAL BASIS OF LOVE

Love is not just a feeling; it is also a physiological state driven by a complex interplay of hormones and neurotransmitters. Oxytocin, often referred to as the "love hormone," plays a crucial role in bonding and attachment, while dopamine is associated with the pleasure and reward mechanisms that make love feel so exhilarating. This chapter will explore the neurobiological underpinnings of love, examining how these chemicals influence our emotions and behaviors.

The Role of Neurotransmitters in Love

Neurotransmitters are chemical messengers that transmit signals between nerve cells (neurons) in the brain and throughout the nervous system. They play a vital role in regulating various physiological and psychological processes, including emotions, mood, and behavior. In the context of love, several key neurotransmitters are involved:

1. Dopamine:

- Function:

- Dopamine is a neurotransmitter associated with the brain's reward and pleasure centers. It plays a crucial role in motivation, arousal, and reinforcement of behaviors.

- Impact on Love:

- When individuals fall in love, dopamine levels increase, leading to feelings of euphoria, excitement, and pleasure. This heightened dopamine activity reinforces the behaviors and interactions associated with love, making them feel rewarding and desirable. The initial stages of romantic love are often characterized by intense dopamine-driven exhilaration and obsession with the loved one.

2. Serotonin:

- Function:

- Serotonin is a neurotransmitter that regulates mood, appetite, sleep, and social behavior. It contributes to feelings of well-being and emotional stability.

- Impact on Love:

- During the early stages of romantic love, serotonin levels may decrease, leading to increased mood swings, obsessive thoughts, and preoccupation with the loved one. Over time, as relationships stabilize and move into more mature phases, serotonin levels return to normal, contributing to a sense of calm and emotional equilibrium.

3. Norepinephrine:

- Function:

- Norepinephrine is a neurotransmitter involved in the body's fight-or-flight response, regulating alertness, arousal, and attention.

- Impact on Love:

- Norepinephrine levels increase during the early stages of love, leading to heightened arousal, increased heart rate, and physical symptoms such as butterflies in the stomach. This neurotransmitter contributes to the excitement and nervous energy often experienced in the initial phases of a romantic relationship.

The Role of Hormones in Love

Hormones are chemical substances produced by glands in the endocrine system that regulate various bodily functions and processes. In the context of love, several key hormones are involved:

1. Oxytocin:

- Function:

- Oxytocin, often referred to as the "love hormone" or "bonding hormone," is produced in the hypothalamus and released by the pituitary gland. It plays a crucial role in social bonding, attachment, and trust.

- Impact on Love:

- Oxytocin is released during physical touch, such as hugging, kissing, and sexual activity, promoting feelings of closeness and bonding between partners. It is also released during childbirth and breastfeeding, strengthening the bond between mother and child. Oxytocin enhances feelings of trust, empathy, and emotional connection, contributing to the deep emotional bonds characteristic of long-term relationships.

2. Vasopressin:

- Function:

- Vasopressin is a hormone associated with water retention and blood pressure regulation. It also plays a role in social behavior and bonding.

- Impact on Love:

- Vasopressin is involved in pair-bonding and monogamous behaviors, particularly in males. Studies on animals, such as prairie voles, have shown that vasopressin contributes to the formation of long-term monogamous bonds. In humans, vasopressin is believed to promote commitment, loyalty, and protective behaviors within romantic relationships.

3. Testosterone and Estrogen:

- Function:

- Testosterone and estrogen are sex hormones that regulate sexual development, reproductive functions, and secondary sexual characteristics.

- Impact on Love:

- Testosterone is associated with sexual desire, aggression, and competitive behaviors. Higher levels of testosterone can increase libido and sexual attraction. Estrogen contributes to sexual receptivity and attraction. Both hormones play a role in the initial stages of romantic attraction and sexual chemistry between partners.

The Phases of Love and Their Biological Correlates

Love can be broadly categorized into different phases, each with distinct biological and psychological characteristics:

1. Lust:

- Biological Basis:

- Lust is driven primarily by the sex hormones testosterone and estrogen. These hormones increase sexual desire and attraction, motivating individuals to seek out potential mates.

- Psychological Experience:

- Lust is characterized by intense physical attraction, sexual desire, and a focus on physical appearance and sexual chemistry.

2. Attraction:

- Biological Basis:

- The attraction phase is marked by elevated levels of dopamine, norepinephrine, and low levels of serotonin. These neurotransmitters create feelings of excitement, euphoria, and obsessive thinking about the loved one.

- Psychological Experience:

- Attraction involves emotional arousal, infatuation, and a preoccupation with the partner. Individuals may experience increased energy, decreased need for sleep, and heightened focus on the relationship.

3. Attachment:

- Biological Basis:

- Attachment is mediated by the hormones oxytocin and vasopressin. These hormones promote long-term bonding, emotional closeness, and a sense of security and stability within the relationship.

- Psychological Experience:

- Attachment is characterized by deep emotional connection, trust, and commitment. Partners feel a sense of comfort, safety, and mutual support, fostering long-term relationship satisfaction.

The Role of the Brain in Love

Different regions of the brain are involved in the experience of love, each contributing to the complex interplay of emotions, behaviors, and physiological responses:

1. The Limbic System:

- Function:

- The limbic system, including structures such as the amygdala, hippocampus, and hypothalamus, is involved in regulating emotions, memory, and motivation.

- Impact on Love:

- The limbic system plays a central role in the emotional and motivational aspects of love. The amygdala is involved in processing emotional responses, while the hypothalamus regulates the release of love-related hormones such as oxytocin and vasopressin.

2. The Prefrontal Cortex:

- Function:

- The prefrontal cortex is responsible for higher-order cognitive functions such as decision-making, planning, and self-regulation.

- Impact on Love:

- The prefrontal cortex helps individuals navigate complex social interactions and make decisions about relationships. It is involved in assessing the long-term potential of a partner and regulating impulsive behaviors associated with attraction and lust.

3. The Ventral Tegmental Area (VTA):

- Function:

- The VTA is a key component of the brain's reward system, involved in the release of dopamine and the regulation of pleasure and reward.

- Impact on Love:

- The VTA is highly active during the early stages of romantic love, contributing to feelings of euphoria, motivation, and reinforcement of romantic behaviors.

The Evolutionary Perspective on Love

From an evolutionary standpoint, love and attachment behaviors have developed to promote reproductive success and the survival of offspring. The biological mechanisms underlying love can be understood in the context of their adaptive value:

1. Mate Selection:

- Purpose:

- Love and attraction facilitate mate selection, helping individuals choose partners with favorable genetic traits and reproductive potential.

- Biological Basis:

- Sexual attraction and lust are driven by sex hormones that enhance reproductive success by motivating individuals to seek out and engage with potential mates.

2. Pair-Bonding:

- Purpose:

- Long-term pair-bonding increases the likelihood of successful offspring rearing by providing a stable, supportive environment for children.

- Biological Basis:

- Hormones such as oxytocin and vasopressin promote bonding and attachment, fostering long-term commitment and cooperative parenting behaviors.

3. Parental Investment:

- Purpose:

- Strong emotional bonds between parents and children ensure that offspring receive the care, protection, and resources needed for survival and development.

- Biological Basis:

- Oxytocin plays a critical role in maternal bonding and caregiving behaviors, strengthening the emotional connection between parents and their children.

Understanding the biological basis of love provides valuable insights into the complex interplay of hormones, neurotransmitters, and brain regions that drive our emotions and behaviors. The physiological processes underlying love are deeply intertwined with our evolutionary history, shaping our capacity for attachment, bonding, and reproductive success.

As we continue our exploration of the psychology of love, we will delve into various psychological theories and their implications for understanding human relationships. By integrating insights from biological, psychological, and social perspectives, we can gain a comprehensive understanding of the profound and transformative power of love in our lives.

Love is not merely a subjective experience or an abstract emotion; it is also deeply rooted in our biology. The physiological state of love is driven by a complex interplay of hormones and neurotransmitters that influence our emotions and behaviors. By examining these biochemical processes, we can gain a better understanding of why love is such a powerful and enduring aspect of the human experience.

The Role of Oxytocin

Oxytocin, often referred to as the "love hormone," is pivotal in the formation and maintenance of bonds between individuals. This hormone is released in large quantities during childbirth and breastfeeding, promoting maternal bonding with the infant. However, oxytocin is not limited to parent-child interactions; it also plays a significant role in romantic relationships. When individuals engage in intimate behaviors such as hugging, kissing, or sexual activity, oxytocin levels increase, fostering feelings of closeness and attachment. This hormonal surge enhances trust and reduces fear, making individuals more likely to form deep, enduring bonds with their partners.

Dopamine and the Pleasure of Love

Dopamine is another critical neurotransmitter involved in the experience of love. Often associated with the brain's reward system, dopamine is released in response to pleasurable activities, including those related to romantic love. The early stages of a romantic relationship are often marked by heightened levels of dopamine, which create feelings of euphoria, excitement, and intense focus on the partner. This biochemical response explains the "honeymoon phase" that many couples experience, characterized by obsessive thoughts about the partner and a strong desire to spend time together. The pleasure and reward mechanisms driven by dopamine encourage individuals to pursue and maintain romantic relationships.

The Role of Serotonin

Serotonin, a neurotransmitter that contributes to feelings of well-being and happiness, also plays a role in romantic love. Interestingly, serotonin levels in individuals who are newly in love tend to be lower than usual, resembling the chemical imbalance seen in obsessive-compulsive disorder. This decrease in serotonin may explain the obsessive thoughts and behaviors often observed in the early stages of romantic relationships. As the relationship stabilizes and matures, serotonin levels normalize, contributing to a more balanced and stable emotional state.

Evolutionary Theories of Love

Understanding the biological basis of love also involves exploring its evolutionary roots. Evolutionary theories suggest that romantic love evolved to promote pair bonding and reproductive success. In the context of human evolution, forming strong, long-lasting bonds with a mate would have provided several advantages. Stable pair bonds would have facilitated cooperative parenting, ensuring that offspring received the care and protection needed for survival. Additionally, strong bonds between partners would have increased the chances of mutual support and resource sharing, enhancing the overall fitness and survival of both individuals and their offspring.

One prominent evolutionary theory is the attachment theory, which posits that early human ancestors who formed strong emotional bonds with their mates had a better chance of raising successful offspring. This theory is supported by the presence of attachment behaviors in both humans and other mammals, indicating a deep-rooted biological mechanism for forming bonds. The drive to bond with a mate and provide care for offspring is thus seen as a crucial factor in the evolutionary success of our species.

The Universality of Love

The biological underpinnings of love help explain why it is a universal phenomenon, transcending cultures and societies. Regardless of cultural differences, the fundamental processes driving love are consistent across humanity. The release of oxytocin, dopamine, and serotonin in response to love-related stimuli is a shared human experience, reinforcing the idea that love is an integral part of the human condition. This universality underscores the importance of love in human social structures and its role in fostering cooperation, social cohesion, and emotional well-being.

Love, while often perceived as a purely emotional or psychological experience, is deeply rooted in our biology. The interplay of hormones and neurotransmitters like oxytocin, dopamine, and serotonin drives the emotions and behaviors associated with love, influencing how we form and maintain relationships. Evolutionary theories provide further insight into the origins and functions of love, highlighting its role in promoting pair bonding and reproductive success. By understanding the biological basis of love, we can appreciate its profound impact on our lives and its enduring significance in the human experience.

CHAPTER 03

PSYCHOLOGICAL THEORIES OF LOVE

Understanding love through the lens of psychology provides valuable insights into how this complex emotion shapes our behavior and relationships. Among the numerous theories developed to explain love, Sternberg's Triangular Theory of Love stands out for its comprehensive approach. This theory posits that love is composed of three components: intimacy, passion, and commitment. Different combinations of these components result in different types of love, such as romantic love, companionate love, and consummate love. In this chapter, we will explore Sternberg's Triangular Theory of Love in detail, examine other psychological theories of love, and discuss their implications for understanding human relationships.

Sternberg's Triangular Theory of Love

Psychologist Robert Sternberg introduced his Triangular Theory of Love in the late 1980s. According to

Sternberg, love can be understood by examining three core components: intimacy, passion, and commitment. These components can be combined in various ways to form different types of love.

1. Intimacy:

- Intimacy refers to feelings of closeness, connectedness, and bondedness in a loving relationship. It involves emotional support, sharing, and a sense of togetherness. Intimacy is the foundation of deep, meaningful relationships and contributes to the overall satisfaction and stability of a partnership.

2. Passion:

- Passion involves physical attraction, sexual desire, and the drive for romantic and physical connection. It is characterized by intense emotions and physiological arousal. Passion is often the initial spark that draws individuals together in romantic relationships.

3. Commitment:

- Commitment refers to the decision to maintain a long-term relationship and the willingness to work through challenges and obstacles. It involves a conscious choice to remain with a partner and build a future together. Commitment provides stability and security in a relationship.

Sternberg proposed that the combination of these three components can create different types of love:

- Liking (Intimacy Alone):

- Relationships characterized by high intimacy but low passion and commitment. These relationships are often seen in close friendships where individuals share a deep emotional bond without romantic or long-term intentions.

- Infatuation (Passion Alone):

- Relationships driven by high passion but lacking intimacy and commitment. Infatuation often occurs in the early stages of a romantic relationship, where physical attraction and desire are strong, but emotional closeness and long-term plans have not yet developed.

- Empty Love (Commitment Alone):

- Relationships where commitment is present without intimacy or passion. This type of love may be seen in long-term marriages or partnerships that have lost their emotional and physical connection but remain together out of obligation or convenience.

- Romantic Love (Intimacy + Passion):

- Relationships that combine intimacy and passion but lack commitment. Romantic love involves both emotional closeness and physical attraction, creating a deep and fulfilling connection. However, without commitment, these relationships may be unstable or short-lived.

- Companionate Love (Intimacy + Commitment):

- Relationships characterized by high intimacy and commitment but low passion. Companionate love is often seen in long-term partnerships where the initial passion has waned, but emotional closeness and dedication to each other remain strong.

- Fatuous Love (Passion + Commitment):

- Relationships that combine passion and commitment but lack intimacy. Fatuous love involves a strong physical and romantic connection, along with a commitment to the relationship, but without the deep emotional bond that comes with intimacy.

- Consummate Love (Intimacy + Passion + Commitment):

- The ideal form of love that combines all three components: intimacy, passion, and commitment. Consummate love represents a balanced, fulfilling, and enduring relationship that encompasses emotional closeness, physical attraction, and a long-term commitment to each other.

Other Psychological Theories of Love

While Sternberg's Triangular Theory of Love provides a comprehensive framework for understanding love, other psychological theories offer additional perspectives on this complex emotion. Here, we will explore some of these theories and their contributions to our understanding of love.

1. Attachment Theory:

- Attachment theory, developed by John Bowlby and expanded by Mary Ainsworth, explores how early relationships with caregivers shape our ability to form and maintain love relationships in adulthood. According to this theory, individuals develop attachment styles based on their early experiences, which influence their approach to relationships:

- Secure Attachment: Individuals with a secure attachment style tend to have positive views of themselves and others. They are comfortable with intimacy and dependence on others, leading to healthy and stable relationships.

- Anxious Attachment: Individuals with an anxious attachment style may have a negative view of themselves and a positive view of others. They often seek high levels of intimacy and approval but may be overly dependent on their partners and fear abandonment.

- Avoidant Attachment: Individuals with an avoidant attachment style may have a positive view of themselves but a negative view of others. They often avoid intimacy and dependence, leading to difficulties in forming close relationships.

- Disorganized Attachment: Individuals with a disorganized attachment style may have a negative view of themselves and others. They may exhibit inconsistent or erratic behaviors in relationships, stemming from unresolved trauma or loss.

2. The Five Love Languages:

- Dr. Gary Chapman proposed that people express and receive love in five distinct ways, known as love languages. Understanding one's own love language and that of a partner can enhance communication and strengthen relationships:

- Words of Affirmation: Expressing love through verbal compliments, encouragement, and expressions of appreciation.

- Acts of Service: Demonstrating love through helpful actions and gestures that make a partner's life easier.

- Receiving Gifts: Showing love through thoughtful gifts that convey care and thoughtfulness.

- Quality Time: Spending meaningful time together, giving undivided attention and creating shared experiences.

- Physical Touch: Expressing love through physical affection, such as hugging, kissing, and holding hands.

3. Social Exchange Theory:

- Social exchange theory, developed by John Thibaut and Harold Kelley, posits that relationships are formed and maintained based on a cost-benefit analysis. Individuals seek to maximize rewards (e.g., love, support, companionship) and minimize costs (e.g., conflict, stress, effort) in their relationships. Satisfaction and commitment in a relationship are influenced by the perceived balance of rewards and costs, as well as comparisons to alternative relationships.

4. Equity Theory:

- Equity theory, developed by Elaine Hatfield, suggests that individuals are most satisfied in relationships where there is a perceived sense of fairness and balance. People compare the ratio of their contributions (e.g., time, effort, resources) to their rewards (e.g., love, support, satisfaction) with those of their partner. Relationships perceived as equitable are more likely to be satisfying and stable, while perceived inequities can lead to dissatisfaction and conflict.

Implications for Understanding Human Relationships

The psychological theories of love discussed in this chapter offer valuable insights into the dynamics of human relationships. By understanding the different components of love and the factors that influence our experiences of love, we can navigate our relationships more effectively and foster healthier, more fulfilling connections.

1. Self-Awareness:

- Understanding one's own attachment style, love language, and needs can enhance self-awareness and improve relationship satisfaction. By recognizing personal patterns and preferences, individuals can communicate more effectively with their partners and address potential challenges.

2. Communication:

- Effective communication is crucial for building and maintaining healthy relationships. By understanding and expressing love in ways that resonate with a partner's love language, individuals can strengthen their emotional connection and foster mutual understanding.

3. Conflict Resolution:

- Understanding the psychological dynamics of love can help individuals navigate conflicts and challenges in their relationships. By recognizing the underlying needs and motivations that drive behavior, partners can work together to find solutions and maintain a sense of fairness and equity.

4. Long-Term Commitment:

- Building and sustaining long-term commitment requires a balance of intimacy, passion, and dedication. By nurturing all three components of love, individuals can create stable, enduring relationships that provide emotional fulfillment and support.

Love is a multifaceted emotion that shapes our behavior, relationships, and overall well-being. Sternberg's Triangular Theory of Love, along with other psychological theories, provides a comprehensive framework for understanding the different components and dynamics of love. By exploring these theories, we gain valuable insights into how love develops, evolves, and influences our lives.

As we continue our journey through the psychology of love, we will delve deeper into the various types of love, their impact on mental health, and practical strategies for nurturing healthy, fulfilling relationships. Understanding the psychological underpinnings of love can enrich our own lives and help us build stronger, more meaningful connections with others.

Psychological Theories of Love

Attachment Theory: Originally developed by John Bowlby and later expanded by Mary Ainsworth, attachment theory suggests that the bond between infants and their primary caregivers forms the basis for later relationships. Secure, anxious, and avoidant attachment styles can significantly impact romantic relationships in adulthood.

Introduction to Attachment Theory

Attachment theory is a psychological model that explains how the early relationships we form with our caregivers influence our social, emotional, and relational development throughout life. John Bowlby, a British psychoanalyst, first introduced the concept in the mid-20th century, emphasizing the importance of the child's relationship with their primary caregiver in shaping their emotional and social development. Mary Ainsworth, a developmental psychologist, expanded on Bowlby's work through her empirical research, particularly her "Strange Situation" study, which identified different attachment styles in infants.

Attachment theory posits that the bonds formed between infants and their primary caregivers serve as a prototype for future relationships. These early attachment experiences influence how individuals perceive themselves and others, affecting their ability to form and maintain healthy, secure relationships in adulthood.

Types of Attachment Styles

1. Secure Attachment:

- Characteristics:

- Individuals with a secure attachment style tend to have a positive view of themselves and others. They are comfortable with intimacy and dependency in relationships and are generally trusting and empathetic.

- Development:

- Secure attachment develops when caregivers are consistently responsive, reliable, and emotionally available. Infants learn that their needs will be met, fostering a sense of safety and trust.

- Impact on Adult Relationships:

- Adults with secure attachment styles are typically able to form healthy, stable, and satisfying relationships. They are comfortable with closeness and independence and can communicate effectively and resolve conflicts constructively.

2. Anxious Attachment:

- Characteristics:

- Individuals with an anxious attachment style often have a negative view of themselves and a positive view of others. They may seek high levels of intimacy, approval, and validation from their partners and are often preoccupied with fears of abandonment or rejection.

- Development:

- Anxious attachment can develop when caregivers are inconsistent in their responsiveness and availability. Infants may experience uncertainty about whether their needs will be met, leading to heightened anxiety and clinginess.

- Impact on Adult Relationships:

- Adults with anxious attachment styles may experience intense emotional highs and lows in relationships. They may be overly dependent on their partners, struggle with jealousy and insecurity, and have difficulty trusting their partner's love and commitment.

3. Avoidant Attachment:

- Characteristics:

- Individuals with an avoidant attachment style often have a positive view of themselves but a negative view of others. They may value independence and self-sufficiency, often avoiding intimacy and emotional closeness in relationships.

- Development:

- Avoidant attachment can develop when caregivers are emotionally unavailable, unresponsive, or rejecting. Infants learn to self-soothe and may become emotionally distant as a way to protect themselves from rejection or disappointment.

- Impact on Adult Relationships:

- Adults with avoidant attachment styles may struggle with intimacy and emotional closeness. They may prioritize independence over relationship needs, avoid vulnerability, and have difficulty forming deep, meaningful connections.

4. Disorganized Attachment:

- Characteristics:

- Individuals with a disorganized attachment style often exhibit a mix of anxious and avoidant behaviors. They may have a negative view of themselves and others and display inconsistent, erratic, or contradictory behaviors in relationships.

- Development:

- Disorganized attachment can develop in the context of trauma, abuse, or neglect, where caregivers are a source of both comfort and fear. Infants may experience confusion and disorientation, leading to a lack of coherent strategy for seeking comfort and security.

- Impact on Adult Relationships:

- Adults with disorganized attachment styles may experience significant challenges in relationships. They may struggle with emotional regulation, exhibit unpredictable behaviors, and have difficulty establishing trust and safety in relationships.

The Strange Situation: Ainsworth's Contribution

Mary Ainsworth's "Strange Situation" study was a groundbreaking empirical research that expanded on Bowlby's attachment theory. The study involved observing infants' behaviors in a series of structured episodes, including separations and reunions with their primary caregiver. Ainsworth identified three main attachment styles (secure, anxious, and avoidant) based on the infants' responses to these episodes.

1. Secure Attachment:

- Infants with a secure attachment used their caregiver as a secure base from which to explore their environment. They were visibly distressed when the caregiver left but were quickly comforted and calmed upon their return.

2. Anxious Attachment:

- Infants with anxious attachment exhibited heightened distress during separations and were not easily comforted upon the caregiver's return. They often displayed clinginess and resistance to being comforted, indicating anxiety and insecurity.

3. Avoidant Attachment:

- Infants with avoidant attachment showed little distress during separations and avoided or ignored the caregiver upon their return. They often appeared emotionally distant and self-reliant, indicating a lack of trust in the caregiver's availability.

4. Disorganized Attachment:

- Later research identified a fourth attachment style, disorganized attachment, characterized by a lack of coherent response to separations and reunions. Infants with disorganized attachment displayed confusing and contradictory behaviors, such as approaching the caregiver while simultaneously avoiding eye contact.

Implications for Romantic Relationships

Attachment styles formed in early childhood have profound implications for romantic relationships in adulthood. Understanding these attachment patterns can help individuals and couples navigate their relationship dynamics more effectively.

1. Secure Attachment in Romantic Relationships:

- Adults with secure attachment styles are generally comfortable with intimacy and independence. They are capable of forming deep emotional connections and are more likely to experience stable, satisfying relationships. They tend to communicate openly, resolve conflicts constructively, and provide mutual support and reassurance.

2. Anxious Attachment in Romantic Relationships:

- Adults with anxious attachment styles may struggle with feelings of insecurity and fear of abandonment. They may seek constant reassurance and validation from their partners, leading to behaviors that can strain the relationship. These individuals may benefit from developing self-soothing techniques and building self-esteem to reduce dependency on their partners for emotional security.

3. Avoidant Attachment in Romantic Relationships:

- Adults with avoidant attachment styles may prioritize independence and self-reliance, often avoiding emotional intimacy and vulnerability. They may struggle with expressing their feelings and may distance themselves in times of stress. Building trust and gradually increasing emotional openness can help avoidant individuals form more satisfying connections.

4. Disorganized Attachment in Romantic Relationships:

- Adults with disorganized attachment styles may experience significant challenges in relationships, including difficulty trusting others and regulating emotions. Therapy and support can be crucial for individuals with disorganized attachments to heal from past traumas and develop healthier relational patterns.

Attachment Theory and Relationship Interventions

Understanding attachment theory can inform therapeutic interventions and strategies for improving relationships. By addressing attachment-related issues, individuals and couples can work towards healthier, more secure connections.

1. Individual Therapy:

- Therapy can help individuals explore their attachment histories and understand how early experiences shape their current relational patterns. Therapeutic approaches, such as cognitive-behavioral therapy (CBT) and attachment-based therapy, can facilitate self-awareness, emotional regulation, and the development of secure attachment behaviors.

2. Couples Therapy:

- Couples therapy can provide a safe space for partners to explore their attachment dynamics and address relational challenges. Therapists can help couples improve communication, build trust, and develop strategies for supporting each other's attachment needs.

3. Self-Help Strategies:

- Individuals can enhance their attachment security by practicing self-awareness, self-compassion, and effective communication. Reading books on attachment theory, attending workshops, and engaging in mindfulness practices can also support personal growth and relational health.

Attachment theory provides a profound understanding of how early relationships with caregivers shape our ability to form and maintain love relationships in adulthood. Secure, anxious, avoidant, and disorganized attachment styles each have distinct characteristics and implications for romantic relationships. By exploring and addressing these attachment patterns, individuals and couples can work towards healthier, more fulfilling connections.

As we continue our exploration of the psychology of love, we will delve deeper into other psychological theories and their implications for understanding human relationships. By integrating insights from various theoretical perspectives, we can gain a comprehensive understanding of the complex, multifaceted nature of love and its impact on our lives.

Behavioral Theories: Understanding Love through Reinforcement and Learning

Behavioral theories offer a unique perspective on love, emphasizing the role of reinforcement, learning, and environmental influences in shaping emotional and relational experiences. Unlike theories that focus on internal processes and attachment styles, behavioral theories consider love as a learned behavior influenced by external factors and positive reinforcement.

Introduction to Behavioral Theories

Behavioral theories of love are rooted in the principles of behaviorism, a psychological approach that emphasizes observable behaviors and their relationships with the environment. Behaviorists believe that behaviors, including emotional responses, are shaped by reinforcement and punishment. These theories suggest that love develops through a series of positive interactions and experiences that reinforce affectionate behaviors.

Key figures in behaviorism, such as B.F. Skinner and John Watson laid the groundwork for understanding how reinforcement and learning influence behavior. In the context of love, behavioral theories propose that affectionate behaviors are reinforced by positive outcomes, leading to the development and maintenance of love relationships.

The Role of Reinforcement in Love

Reinforcement is a fundamental concept in behaviorism, referring to any event that strengthens or increases the likelihood of a behavior. In the context of love, reinforcement can occur through various positive experiences and interactions with a partner.

1. Positive Reinforcement:

- Positive reinforcement involves presenting a desirable stimulus following a behavior, increasing the likelihood of that behavior being repeated. In romantic relationships, positive reinforcement can take many forms, such as compliments, physical affection, gifts, and acts of kindness. When partners consistently experience positive reinforcement, they are more likely to develop and sustain feelings of love and affection.

2. Negative Reinforcement:

- Negative reinforcement involves removing an aversive stimulus following a behavior, increasing the likelihood of that behavior being repeated. In relationships, negative reinforcement can occur when partners help each other alleviate stress or discomfort. For example, a partner might provide comfort and support during a difficult time, reinforcing the bond between them.

Learning Love through Social Interaction

Behavioral theories also emphasize the importance of social learning in the development of love. Social learning theory, developed by Albert Bandura, suggests that individuals learn behaviors through observation, imitation, and modeling. In the context of love, social learning theory posits that individuals learn how to express and experience love by observing the behaviors of others, particularly significant role models such as parents, peers, and media figures.

1. Observational Learning:

- Observational learning occurs when individuals observe and imitate the behaviors of others. In romantic relationships, individuals may learn affectionate behaviors by observing how their parents or other couples express love and affection. Positive interactions and expressions of love observed in others can influence how individuals behave in their own relationships.

2. Modeling:

- Modeling involves imitating the behaviors of role models. In the context of love, individuals may model their romantic behaviors based on the examples set by significant others. For instance, if a person observes their parents demonstrating affectionate and supportive behaviors, they are more likely to replicate those behaviors in their own relationships.

Behavioral Interventions in Relationship Therapy

Behavioral theories provide a framework for understanding how positive reinforcement and learning influence love and offer practical interventions for improving relationships. Behavioral interventions in relationship therapy focus on enhancing positive interactions and reducing negative behaviors through various techniques.

1. Behavioral Couples Therapy (BCT):

- Behavioral Couples Therapy is an evidence-based approach that focuses on improving communication, increasing positive interactions, and reducing negative behaviors in relationships. BCT techniques include teaching couples effective communication skills, encouraging positive reinforcement through affectionate behaviors, and setting goals for positive changes in the relationship.

2. Positive Reinforcement Strategies:

- Therapists may encourage couples to engage in behaviors that reinforce love and affection, such as expressing gratitude, giving compliments, and spending quality time together. By increasing the frequency of positive interactions, couples can strengthen their emotional bond and enhance relationship satisfaction.

3. Social Learning Interventions:

- Social learning interventions involve teaching couples new behaviors through observation and modeling. Therapists may use role-playing exercises to demonstrate effective communication and problem-solving skills, allowing couples to practice and internalize these behaviors.

Criticisms and Limitations of Behavioral Theories

While behavioral theories provide valuable insights into the role of reinforcement and learning in love, they also face criticisms and limitations. Some of the main critiques include:

1. Reductionism:

- Behavioral theories have been criticized for being overly reductionistic, reducing complex emotional experiences to simple behaviors and reinforcement patterns. Critics argue that love involves intricate cognitive and emotional processes that cannot be fully explained by observable behaviors alone.

2. Neglect of Internal Processes:

- Behavioral theories tend to focus on external behaviors and reinforcement, often neglecting the internal cognitive and emotional processes that contribute to love. Critics suggest that a comprehensive understanding of love requires integrating behavioral perspectives with cognitive and emotional theories.

3. Contextual Influences:

- Behavioral theories may not fully account for the broader social and cultural contexts that influence love and relationships. Factors such as cultural norms, societal expectations, and individual differences can significantly impact how love is expressed and experienced.

Integrating Behavioral Theories with Other Perspectives

Despite their limitations, behavioral theories offer valuable insights into the role of reinforcement and learning in love. Integrating behavioral perspectives with other psychological theories can provide a more comprehensive understanding of love and relationships.

1. Combining Behavioral and Attachment Theories:

- Integrating behavioral theories with attachment theory can offer a more holistic view of love. While attachment theory emphasizes the importance of early relationships and internal attachment styles, behavioral theories highlight the role of reinforcement and learning in shaping behaviors. Together, these perspectives can provide a richer understanding of how early experiences and ongoing interactions influence love.

2. Incorporating Cognitive and Emotional Theories:

- Combining behavioral theories with cognitive and emotional theories can provide a more nuanced understanding of love. Cognitive theories focus on the role of thoughts and beliefs in shaping emotions and behaviors, while emotional theories explore the complex emotional experiences associated with love. Integrating these perspectives with behavioral theories can offer a more comprehensive view of how love develops and is maintained.

Behavioral theories provide a unique perspective on love, emphasizing the role of reinforcement and learning in shaping emotional and relational experiences. By focusing on observable behaviors and their relationships with the environment, these theories highlight how positive interactions and social learning influence the development and maintenance of love.

While behavioral theories have limitations and criticisms, they offer valuable insights that can inform therapeutic interventions and strategies for improving relationships. By integrating behavioral perspectives with other psychological theories, we can gain a more comprehensive understanding of the complex, multifaceted nature of love and its impact on our lives.

As we continue our exploration of the psychology of love, we will delve into other psychological theories and their implications for understanding human relationships. By integrating insights from various theoretical perspectives, we can gain a deeper appreciation of the profound and transformative power of love.

CHAPTER 04

THE IMPACT OF LOVE ON MENTAL HEALTH AND WELL-BEING

Love, in its various forms, profoundly influences mental health and overall well-being. Positive, loving relationships can provide emotional support, reduce stress, and enhance life satisfaction, while troubled or unrequited love can lead to emotional distress and mental health challenges. This chapter delves into the ways love affects mental health, exploring both the beneficial and potentially harmful aspects of this powerful emotion.

The Benefits of Love on Mental Health

1. Emotional Support and Resilience:

- Support Systems:

- Loving relationships, whether romantic, familial, or platonic, provide essential emotional support. Knowing there is someone who cares and is available to listen and offer help can significantly enhance emotional resilience.

- Coping Mechanisms:

- Love and support from close relationships equip individuals with better-coping mechanisms for dealing with life's challenges. This support can mitigate the impact of stressors, reducing the likelihood of developing mental health issues such as anxiety and depression.

2. Stress Reduction:

- Oxytocin and Stress:

- Physical affection, such as hugging and cuddling, releases oxytocin, which has been shown to reduce stress levels by lowering cortisol, the stress hormone. This hormone also promotes a sense of calm and security, further buffering against stress.

- Social Support:

- Having a strong support system can reduce the perception of stress and improve one's ability to manage stressful situations. The emotional reassurance and practical help provided by loved ones play a crucial role in stress management.

3. Enhanced Self-Esteem and Life Satisfaction:

- Affirmation and Validation:

- Loving relationships provide affirmation and validation, boosting self-esteem and self-worth. Feeling valued and appreciated by others contributes to a positive self-image and overall life satisfaction.

- Sense of Belonging:

- Love fosters a sense of belonging and connectedness, which is fundamental to human well-being. This sense of belonging can lead to greater happiness and fulfillment in life.

4. Physical Health Benefits:

- Healthier Lifestyle Choices:

- Individuals in loving relationships often engage in healthier behaviors, such as regular exercise, balanced diets, and avoiding harmful habits like smoking or excessive drinking, due to mutual encouragement and accountability.

- Improved Health Outcomes:

- The stress-reducing effects of love and emotional support are linked to better health outcomes, including lower blood pressure, reduced risk of chronic diseases, and a longer lifespan.

The Challenges of Love on Mental Health

1. Emotional Distress from Troubled Relationships:

- Conflict and Stress:

- Relationships characterized by frequent conflict, lack of communication, or emotional neglect can cause significant stress and emotional distress. Such negative experiences can contribute to anxiety, depression, and other mental health issues.

- Attachment Insecurities:

- Individuals with insecure attachment styles (anxious or avoidant) may struggle with maintaining healthy relationships, leading to ongoing emotional turmoil and relationship dissatisfaction.

2. Heartbreak and Unrequited Love:

- Psychological Impact:

- The end of a relationship or unrequited love can lead to intense emotional pain, grief, and feelings of rejection. This heartbreak can manifest as depression, anxiety, and in severe cases, suicidal thoughts.

- Cognitive and Emotional Repercussions:

- Heartbreak can trigger rumination, where individuals continuously dwell on their loss and perceived failures, exacerbating negative emotions and hindering emotional recovery.

3. Codependency and Loss of Identity:

- Codependent Relationships:

- In codependent relationships, one partner may rely excessively on the other for emotional support and validation, leading to an imbalance in the relationship. This can result in a loss of self-identity and increased emotional dependency.

- Personal Growth Stagnation:

- Codependency can stifle personal growth and self-improvement, as individuals may prioritize the relationship over their own needs and aspirations, leading to diminished self-worth and autonomy.

Strategies for Promoting Healthy Relationships

1. Effective Communication:

- Open and Honest Dialogue:

- Healthy relationships are built on open, honest, and respectful communication. Expressing thoughts, feelings, and concerns transparently helps prevent misunderstandings and fosters emotional intimacy.

- Active Listening:

- Active listening involves fully engaging with the speaker, showing empathy, and providing feedback. This practice enhances mutual understanding and strengthens the emotional connection between partners.

2. Building Trust and Security:

- Consistency and Reliability:

- Trust is established through consistent, reliable behavior. Keeping promises, being dependable, and demonstrating integrity build a strong foundation of trust in relationships.

- Emotional Availability:

- Being emotionally available and responsive to a partner's needs fosters a sense of security and trust. This involves being attentive, empathetic, and supportive during both good and challenging times.

3. Balancing Independence and Togetherness:

- Maintaining Individual Identity:

- While emotional closeness is essential, maintaining individual identities and personal interests is equally important. Encouraging independence and supporting each other's personal growth contribute to a balanced and healthy relationship.

- Quality Time Together:

- Spending quality time together strengthens the emotional bond and fosters shared experiences. Engaging in activities that both partners enjoy and finding common interests can enhance relationship satisfaction.

4. Conflict Resolution Skills:

- Healthy Disagreement:

- Disagreements are natural in any relationship, but how they are handled makes a significant difference. Approaching conflicts with a calm, respectful attitude and seeking mutually agreeable solutions promotes healthier interactions.

- Compromise and Negotiation:

- Effective conflict resolution often involves compromise and negotiation. Being willing to find a middle ground and prioritize the relationship over individual desires can lead to more harmonious and enduring partnerships.

The Role of Therapy and Counseling

1. Couples Therapy:

- Improving Relationship Dynamics:

- Couples therapy provides a structured environment for partners to address issues, improve communication, and strengthen their relationship. Therapists guide couples in exploring underlying problems and developing healthier interaction patterns.

- Rebuilding Trust:

- Therapy can help rebuild trust in relationships damaged by betrayal, infidelity, or other breaches of trust. Through guided exercises and discussions, couples can work towards healing and re-establishing a strong bond.

2. Individual Therapy:

- Self-Awareness and Growth:

- Individual therapy helps individuals understand their own emotional needs, attachment styles, and relationship patterns. This self-awareness can lead to personal growth and improved relationship dynamics.

- Addressing Attachment Issues:

- Therapy can assist individuals in addressing and healing attachment issues that impact their relationships. Understanding and modifying insecure attachment patterns can lead to healthier, more fulfilling relationships.

3. Support Groups:

- Shared Experiences:

- Support groups provide a sense of community and understanding, where individuals can share their experiences and receive validation and support from others facing similar challenges.

- Learning from Others:

- Support groups offer opportunities to learn from others' experiences, gain new perspectives, and develop effective coping strategies for relationship-related issues.

The impact of love on mental health and well-being is profound and multifaceted. While love can provide immense emotional support, reduce stress, and enhance life satisfaction, it can also pose challenges when relationships are troubled or unrequited. Understanding the psychological and biological underpinnings of love can help individuals navigate their relationships more effectively, promoting healthier interactions and fostering emotional resilience. By adopting strategies for building and maintaining healthy relationships and seeking professional support when needed, individuals can enhance their mental health and overall well-being, ensuring that love remains a source of joy and fulfillment in their lives.

THE ROLE OF LOVE IN PERSONA; DEVELOPMENT AND IDENTITY FORMATION

Love is a powerful force in shaping personal development and identity. From early childhood attachments to adult romantic relationships, love influences how we see ourselves, how we interact with others, and how we grow as individuals. This chapter explores how love contributes to personal development and identity formation across different stages of life.

Early Childhood and Attachment

1. Formation of Attachment Styles:

- Secure Attachment:

- Secure attachment forms when caregivers are consistently responsive and nurturing. Children with secure attachments feel safe to explore their environment, knowing they have a reliable support system. This foundation fosters self-confidence and positive social interactions.

- Insecure Attachment:

- Inconsistent or neglectful caregiving can lead to insecure attachment styles. Anxious attachment arises from unpredictability in caregiver responses, leading to clinginess and fear of abandonment. Avoidant attachment results from caregivers being emotionally unavailable, causing children to distance themselves emotionally.

2. Impact on Self-Esteem and Social Skills:

- Self-Worth:

- Children with secure attachment typically develop higher self-esteem and a stronger sense of self-worth. They feel valued and capable, which positively impacts their social interactions and academic performance.

- Interpersonal Relationships:

- Securely attached children are more likely to form healthy relationships with peers and adults. They possess better communication skills, empathy, and the ability to manage conflicts effectively.

Adolescence: Exploring Identity and Relationships

1. Developing Autonomy:

- Parental Influence:

- During adolescence, the influence of parents and primary caregivers continues to play a crucial role in identity formation. Supportive and understanding parents encourage adolescents to explore their identities and develop autonomy.

- Peer Relationships:

- Peer relationships become increasingly significant during adolescence. Friendships and romantic relationships provide opportunities to explore different aspects of identity and learn about intimacy and emotional connection.

2. Romantic Relationships:

- Learning About Love:

- Adolescent romantic relationships are often a first step in learning about love, intimacy, and commitment. These early experiences can shape expectations and behaviors in future relationships.

- Emotional Development:

- Navigating the complexities of romantic relationships during adolescence contributes to emotional development. Adolescents learn to manage emotions, communicate effectively, and build emotional resilience.

Adulthood: Love and Identity Integration

1. Romantic Partnerships:

- Identity and Partnership:

- In adulthood, romantic partnerships play a significant role in shaping identity. These relationships often involve a deeper level of emotional and practical integration, influencing how individuals see themselves and their place in the world.

- Mutual Growth:

- Healthy romantic relationships promote mutual growth and self-improvement. Partners support each other's personal goals and aspirations, contributing to a sense of shared purpose and fulfillment.

2. Parental Love and Identity:

- Parenthood and Self-Concept:

- Becoming a parent significantly impacts identity. Parental love fosters a sense of responsibility, selflessness, and purpose. The experience of raising children can lead to profound personal growth and a reevaluation of one's values and priorities.

- Modeling Behavior:

- Parents serve as role models for their children, influencing their emotional development and attachment styles. The way parents express love and manage relationships sets a template for their children's future interactions.

Love and Self-Actualization

1. Personal Growth through Love:

- Support and Encouragement:

- Loving relationships provide the support and encouragement needed for personal growth. Knowing that someone believes in their potential empowers individuals to pursue their goals and dreams.

- Facing Challenges:

- Love helps individuals face challenges and setbacks with greater resilience. The emotional safety net provided by loving relationships enables people to take risks and grow from their experiences.

2. Self-Discovery and Authenticity:

- Being Seen and Accepted:

- Being loved for who they truly are allows individuals to embrace their authentic selves. This acceptance fosters self-discovery and encourages people to live in alignment with their values and beliefs.

- Transformational Power of Love:

- Love has the power to transform individuals, helping them overcome personal limitations and realize their full potential. The positive influence of love can lead to profound changes in self-perception and life direction.

Challenges in Love and Identity Formation

1. Identity Conflicts in Relationships:

- Balancing Individuality and Togetherness:

- One of the challenges in romantic relationships is balancing individuality with togetherness. Maintaining a sense of self while being part of a partnership requires communication, mutual respect, and personal boundaries.

- Identity Changes:

- Relationships can sometimes lead to identity conflicts, especially if partners have differing goals or values. Navigating these changes requires flexibility, compromise, and a commitment to mutual growth.

2. Impact of Unhealthy Relationships:

- Loss of Self:

- Unhealthy relationships, such as those involving codependency or emotional abuse, can lead to a loss of self. Individuals may sacrifice their own needs and desires to maintain the relationship, resulting in diminished self-worth and identity confusion.

- Recovery and Self-Reclamation:

- Recovering from unhealthy relationships involves reclaiming one's identity and rebuilding self-esteem. This process may include therapy, self-reflection, and establishing healthy boundaries in future relationships.

Love is integral to personal development and identity formation. From early childhood attachments to adult romantic partnerships, love shapes how we see ourselves and interact with the world. Healthy, loving relationships provide the support, validation, and encouragement needed for personal growth and self-actualization. However, challenges in relationships can also impact identity and well-being, highlighting the importance of understanding and fostering healthy relational dynamics. By recognizing the role of love in our development, we can cultivate relationships that enhance our lives and contribute to our ongoing journey of self-discovery and growth.

CHAPTER 06

THE ROLE OF LOVE IN SOCIETY AND CULTURE

Love is not only a personal experience but also a social and cultural phenomenon that shapes and is shaped by the society in which we live. It influences social structures, cultural norms, and collective behaviors. This chapter explores how love operates within societal and cultural contexts, examining its impact on social cohesion, cultural expressions, and societal values.

Love as a Social Glue

1. Social Cohesion:

- Building Communities:

- Love fosters social bonds and community building. Families, friendships, and romantic partnerships are foundational units that contribute to the larger social fabric. These relationships provide support networks that enhance social cohesion and resilience.

- Social Capital:

- The connections formed through loving relationships contribute to social capital, which refers to the networks, norms, and trust that facilitate coordination and cooperation for mutual benefit. Strong social capital enhances community well-being and collective action.

2. Civic Engagement:

- Volunteerism and Altruism:

- Love and empathy drive individuals to engage in volunteerism and altruistic behaviors. Acts of love and kindness, whether within families or extended to the broader community, strengthen societal bonds and promote civic engagement.

- Social Responsibility:

- Love motivates people to care for others and take responsibility for societal well-being. This sense of social responsibility is crucial for addressing social issues and fostering a more compassionate and just society.

Love in Cultural Expressions

1. Art, Literature, and Music:

- Themes of Love:

- Love is a central theme in art, literature, and music across cultures. These expressions capture the beauty, complexity, and diversity of love experiences, resonating with people on a deep emotional level.

- Cultural Narratives:

- Stories of love in cultural narratives reflect societal values, beliefs, and norms. They provide insight into how different cultures understand and experience love, highlighting both universal and culturally specific aspects of this emotion.

2. Rituals and Traditions:

- Celebrating Love:

- Cultural rituals and traditions, such as weddings, anniversaries, and festivals, celebrate love and its significance in society. These events reinforce social bonds and cultural continuity, providing a sense of belonging and shared identity.

- Symbolism and Practices:

- Various symbols and practices, such as exchanging rings or love tokens, express and honor love. These cultural artifacts carry deep emotional meaning and reflect the values and traditions of a community.

Societal Norms and Values

1. Norms Governing Relationships:

- Marriage and Family:

- Societal norms around marriage and family structures are deeply influenced by cultural values. These norms dictate acceptable forms of relationships, roles within families, and expectations for love and commitment.

- Gender Roles:

- Cultural norms often prescribe specific roles for men and women in relationships, impacting how love is expressed and experienced. Challenging and redefining these norms can lead to more equitable and fulfilling relationships.

2. Cultural Variations in Love:

- Individualism vs. Collectivism:

- Cultural orientations towards individualism or collectivism shape how love is perceived and practiced. In individualistic cultures, love may emphasize personal fulfillment and autonomy, whereas in collectivist cultures, love often prioritizes family and community bonds.

- Expressions of Affection:

- Different cultures have unique ways of expressing love and affection. Understanding these variations fosters cross-cultural empathy and appreciation, enriching our understanding of love as a universal yet diverse experience.

Love and Social Change

1. Advocacy and Movements:

- Human Rights and Equality:

- Love can be a powerful motivator for social change and advocacy. Movements for human rights, gender equality, and LGBTQ+ rights are often driven by a deep sense of love and justice, challenging societal norms and promoting inclusivity.

- Peace and Reconciliation:

- Love and forgiveness are essential components of peacebuilding and reconciliation efforts. Societies recovering from conflict or injustice rely on love and empathy to heal divisions and build a more harmonious future.

2. Transformative Potential:

- Personal Transformation:

- Love has the capacity to transform individuals, inspiring them to adopt more compassionate and ethical behaviors. This personal transformation can ripple outwards, influencing societal values and practices.

- Collective Transformation:

- Collective acts of love, such as community service, charitable work, and solidarity in times of crisis, can transform societies. These actions demonstrate the potential of love to drive positive social change and build a more just and compassionate world.

Love's influence extends beyond personal relationships to shape society and culture in profound ways. As a social glue, love enhances social cohesion, civic engagement, and community well-being. Cultural expressions of love in art, literature, and rituals reflect and reinforce societal values and norms. Additionally, love can be a powerful force for social change, advocating for human rights, equality, and reconciliation. Understanding the role of love in society and culture deepens our appreciation of its multifaceted nature and its potential to inspire and transform both individuals and communities. As we continue to explore and celebrate love in its many forms, we contribute to a more compassionate, inclusive, and harmonious world.

CHAPTER 07

LOVE AND MENTAL HEALTH

Love has a profound impact on mental health, influencing emotional well-being, stress levels, and overall psychological resilience. In this chapter, we will explore the relationship between love and mental health, examining how different forms of love—romantic, familial, and platonic—can enhance or detract from mental health. We will also consider the ways in which mental health issues can affect our capacity to give and receive love.

The Positive Impact of Love on Mental Health

1. Emotional Support and Resilience:

- Buffer Against Stress:

- Loving relationships provide a buffer against stress. The emotional support offered by loved ones can help individuals manage stress more effectively, reducing its negative impact on mental health.

- Resilience Building:

- Love enhances resilience by providing a sense of security and belonging. This emotional foundation allows individuals to bounce back from adversity and maintain a positive outlook on life.

2. Improved Self-Esteem and Self-Worth:

- Validation and Acceptance:

- Being loved and valued by others boosts self-esteem and self-worth. The affirmation and acceptance from loved ones reinforce positive self-perception and confidence.

- Encouragement and Motivation:

- Loved ones often provide encouragement and motivation, helping individuals pursue their goals and aspirations. This support fosters a sense of competence and achievement, contributing to mental well-being.

3. Enhanced Emotional Regulation:

- Emotional Safety:

- Loving relationships offer a safe space for expressing emotions. This emotional safety helps individuals process and regulate their feelings, reducing the risk of emotional distress.

- Co-Regulation:

- Partners, family members, and close friends can assist in co-regulation, where they help each other manage and stabilize emotions. This mutual support enhances emotional balance and psychological stability.

The Negative Impact of Love on Mental Health

1. Toxic Relationships:

- Emotional Abuse and Manipulation:

- Toxic relationships characterized by emotional abuse, manipulation, or control can severely impact mental health. These relationships can lead to anxiety, depression, and a diminished sense of self-worth.

- Codependency:

- Codependent relationships, where one partner relies excessively on the other for emotional support and validation, can create an unhealthy dynamic. This dependency can hinder personal growth and lead to emotional exhaustion.

2. Loss and Grief:

- Impact of Bereavement:

- The loss of a loved one, whether through death, separation, or divorce, can result in profound grief and emotional pain. Bereavement can trigger depression, anxiety, and other mental health issues.

- Coping with Heartbreak:

- Romantic heartbreak can lead to significant emotional distress, affecting self-esteem and mental well-being. The end of a relationship often requires a period of emotional healing and adjustment.

3. Unresolved Attachment Issues:

- Attachment Insecurity:

- Individuals with insecure attachment styles may struggle with trust, intimacy, and emotional regulation in relationships. These unresolved attachment issues can contribute to ongoing mental health challenges.

- Fear of Abandonment:

- Fear of abandonment, often stemming from early attachment experiences, can create anxiety and insecurity in relationships. This fear can lead to unhealthy relational patterns and emotional instability.

The Interplay Between Love and Mental Health Disorders

1. Mental Health Disorders Affecting Love:

- Depression:

- Depression can impact an individual's capacity to experience and express love. Feelings of worthlessness, lack of interest, and emotional numbness can strain relationships and reduce emotional intimacy.

- Anxiety Disorders:

- Anxiety disorders, including generalized anxiety, social anxiety, and obsessive-compulsive disorder, can affect relationships. Excessive worry, fear of rejection, and compulsive behaviors can create relational tensions.

- Personality Disorders:

- Personality disorders, such as borderline personality disorder and narcissistic personality disorder, can significantly impact relational dynamics. These disorders often involve difficulties with emotional regulation, empathy, and stable relationships.

2. Love as a Healing Force:

- Therapeutic Relationships:

- Therapeutic relationships, characterized by empathy, trust, and unconditional positive regard, can be healing for individuals with mental health disorders. Therapists often provide a model of healthy relational dynamics.

- Supportive Relationships:

- Supportive relationships with family and friends play a crucial role in mental health recovery. These relationships offer emotional support, understanding, and encouragement during difficult times.

3. Interventions and Support:

- Couples Therapy:

- Couples therapy can help partners navigate mental health challenges together. Therapists work with couples to improve communication, resolve conflicts, and strengthen their emotional bond.

- Family Therapy:

- Family therapy addresses relational issues within the family unit. It helps family members understand and support each other, fostering a healthier family dynamic and improved mental health for all members.

Love has a profound impact on mental health, influencing emotional well-being, stress levels, and psychological resilience. Positive, loving relationships provide emotional support, enhance self-esteem, and improve emotional regulation, contributing to overall mental health. Conversely, toxic relationships, loss, and unresolved attachment issues can negatively affect mental well-being. Mental health disorders can also impact relational dynamics, but love can be a powerful healing force, offering support and encouragement during difficult times. By understanding the intricate relationship between love and mental health, we can cultivate healthier relationships and foster emotional well-being for ourselves and those we love.

CHAPTER 08

THE NEUROSCIENCE OF LOVE

Love is deeply rooted in the brain, where complex neural processes and chemical interactions underpin the emotions and behaviors associated with it. Advances in neuroscience have shed light on how love affects the brain and how the brain influences our experience of love. In this chapter, we will explore the neuroscience of love, focusing on the brain regions, neurotransmitters, and hormonal systems involved in the experience of love.

Brain Regions Involved in Love

1. The Limbic System:

- Amygdala:

- The amygdala plays a critical role in processing emotions, including those related to love. It is involved in the formation and storage of emotional memories, which can influence attachment and emotional responses in relationships.

- Hippocampus:

- The hippocampus is essential for forming new memories and connecting emotions to these memories. It helps create and reinforce the emotional bonds associated with love by linking positive experiences with loved ones.

2. The Reward System:

- Ventral Tegmental Area (VTA):

- The VTA is a key component of the brain's reward system and is heavily involved in the feelings of pleasure and motivation associated with love. It releases dopamine, a neurotransmitter that promotes feelings of pleasure and reinforcement.

- Nucleus Accumbens:

- The nucleus accumbens is another crucial part of the reward system. It interacts with the VTA and is involved in the processing of reward and reinforcement, playing a significant role in the feelings of euphoria and excitement often experienced in romantic love.

3. Prefrontal Cortex:

- Decision-Making and Social Behavior:

- The prefrontal cortex is involved in higher-order cognitive functions, including decision-making, social behavior, and impulse control. It helps regulate the emotional and behavioral aspects of love, contributing to rational decision-making in relationships.

4. Insula:

- Emotional Awareness:

- The insula is associated with emotional awareness and empathy. It helps individuals recognize and interpret their own emotions as well as the emotions of others, which is crucial for maintaining healthy and empathetic relationships.

Neurotransmitters and Hormones in Love

1. Dopamine:

- Pleasure and Reward:

- Dopamine is a key neurotransmitter in the brain's reward system. It is released in response to pleasurable stimuli, including interactions with loved ones, reinforcing behaviors that promote bonding and attachment.

- Motivation:

- Dopamine also plays a role in motivation and goal-directed behavior. The anticipation of reward and the pleasure of being with a loved one drive individuals to seek out and maintain loving relationships.

2. Oxytocin:

- Bonding and Attachment:

- Often referred to as the "love hormone," oxytocin is crucial for bonding and attachment. It is released during physical touch, such as hugging, kissing, and sexual activity, promoting feelings of closeness and intimacy.

- Trust and Empathy:

- Oxytocin enhances trust and empathy, which are essential components of healthy relationships. It helps individuals connect with others on a deeper emotional level and fosters cooperative and supportive behaviors.

3. Serotonin:

- Mood Regulation:

- Serotonin is involved in mood regulation and contributes to feelings of well-being and happiness. Balanced serotonin levels are associated with positive mood states, which can enhance relationship satisfaction.

- Obsessive Thoughts:

- Early stages of romantic love are often characterized by obsessive thoughts about the partner. This phenomenon is linked to decreased serotonin levels, similar to those observed in obsessive-compulsive disorder (OCD).

4. Vasopressin:

- Monogamy and Pair Bonding:

- Vasopressin, like oxytocin, plays a role in social bonding and attachment. It is particularly associated with promoting monogamous behaviors and long-term pair bonding, influencing commitment and loyalty in relationships.

Hormonal Influences

1. Testosterone:

- Sexual Desire:

- Testosterone is a hormone that influences sexual desire and attraction. Higher levels of testosterone are associated with increased libido and the pursuit of romantic and sexual relationships.

- Aggression and Competition:

- Testosterone also influences aggression and competitive behaviors, which can play a role in mate selection and rivalry. These behaviors can impact the dynamics of romantic relationships.

2. Estrogen:

- Emotional Sensitivity:

- Estrogen influences emotional sensitivity and mood. It can enhance emotional responsiveness and nurturing behaviors, which are important for maintaining loving relationships.

- Attractiveness:

- Estrogen also affects physical attractiveness and fertility cues, playing a role in mate selection and attraction.

The Neural Basis of Different Types of Love

1. Romantic Love:

- Intense Emotions and Passion:

- Romantic love is characterized by intense emotions and passion, driven by high levels of dopamine and oxytocin. Brain imaging studies show increased activity in the VTA and other reward-related regions during romantic love.

- Obsessive Focus:

- Romantic love often involves obsessive focus on the partner, linked to decreased serotonin levels. This focus can contribute to the intensity and exclusivity of romantic relationships.

2. Parental Love:

- Protective and Nurturing Behaviors:

- Parental love involves protective and nurturing behaviors, driven by high levels of oxytocin and vasopressin. These hormones promote bonding and caregiving, ensuring the survival and well-being of offspring.

- Emotional Bonding:

- The emotional bonding between parents and children is supported by the limbic system, particularly the amygdala and hippocampus, which reinforce the positive experiences and emotional connections associated with caregiving.

3. Platonic Love:

- Trust and Empathy:

- Platonic love, such as friendships, involves trust and empathy, driven by oxytocin and serotonin. These neurotransmitters promote emotional connection, cooperation, and mutual support.

- Social Support:

- Brain regions associated with social behavior, such as the prefrontal cortex and insula, are active during platonic love. These areas help individuals navigate social interactions and maintain supportive relationships.

The neuroscience of love reveals the intricate neural and chemical processes that underpin this powerful emotion. Brain regions such as the limbic system, reward system, and prefrontal cortex, along with neurotransmitters and hormones like dopamine, oxytocin, and serotonin, play crucial roles in shaping our experiences of love. By understanding these neural mechanisms, we gain insight into the biological foundations of love and its profound impact on our emotions and behaviors. This knowledge not only enriches our appreciation of love but also informs approaches to enhancing relationship satisfaction and mental well-being.

CHAPTER 09

LOVE IN THE DIGITAL AGE

The advent of digital technology has revolutionized nearly every aspect of our lives, including the way we experience and express love. The digital age has transformed the landscape of romantic relationships, introducing new dynamics, challenges, and opportunities. This chapter explores the impact of technology on love and relationships, focusing on online dating, social media, and the ways in which digital communication has reshaped our romantic lives.

Online Dating: A New Landscape for Romance

1. The Rise of Dating Apps and Websites

- Importance: Online dating platforms have become a significant means for people to meet potential partners.

- Outcome: These platforms offer a wide range of options, allowing individuals to connect with others based on shared interests, values, and preferences.

2. Accessibility and Convenience

- Importance: Dating apps provide a convenient way to meet new people without geographical constraints.

- Outcome: Users can easily browse profiles, communicate, and arrange meetings, making the process of finding a partner more efficient.

3. Diverse Options and Inclusivity

- Importance: Online dating platforms cater to a diverse range of preferences and identities.

- Outcome: These platforms promote inclusivity, allowing individuals of different sexual orientations, ethnicities, and backgrounds to find compatible partners.

4. Impact on Relationship Formation

- Importance: Online dating changes how relationships are initiated and developed.

- Outcome: The initial stages of relationships often involve digital communication, which can influence the pace and nature of emotional connection.

5. Challenges and Drawbacks

- Importance: Despite its advantages, online dating also presents certain challenges.

- Outcome: Issues such as misrepresentation, superficial judgments, and the paradox of choice can complicate the process of finding a meaningful relationship.

Social Media and Romantic Relationships

1. Connecting and Maintaining Relationships

- Importance: Social media platforms enable continuous communication and connection.

- Outcome: Couples can stay in touch more easily, share experiences, and maintain intimacy despite physical distance.

2. Public Displays of Affection

- Importance: Social media allows couples to publicly display their relationship.

- Outcome: Public sharing can strengthen the bond between partners but may also lead to pressure to present a perfect relationship.

3. Jealousy and Comparison

- Importance: Social media can trigger jealousy and comparison.

- Outcome: Seeing others' idealized portrayals of their relationships can lead to dissatisfaction and insecurity in one's own relationship.

4. Privacy and Boundaries

- Importance: Managing privacy and boundaries on social media is crucial.

- Outcome: Couples need to navigate what to share publicly and what to keep private, balancing transparency with personal boundaries.

Digital Communication and Its Effects

1. Texting and Instant Messaging

- Importance: Digital communication tools have become central to romantic interactions.

- Outcome: Texting and instant messaging allow for frequent and immediate communication, fostering intimacy but also posing risks of miscommunication.

2. Video Calls and Virtual Dates

- Importance: Video calls have become a popular way for couples to connect, especially in long-distance relationships.

- Outcome: Virtual dates and video interactions help maintain emotional closeness despite physical separation.

3. Digital Intimacy and Sexting

- Importance: The digital age has introduced new forms of intimacy, such as sexting.

- Outcome: While sexting can enhance intimacy, it also raises concerns about privacy and consent.

4. Online Conflict and Resolution

- Importance: Digital communication can influence how couples handle conflicts.

- Outcome: Text-based arguments may escalate due to lack of nonverbal cues, but digital tools can also facilitate conflict resolution through thoughtful, written communication.

The Impact of Technology on Relationship Dynamics

1. Increased Connectivity

- Importance: Technology allows for constant connection and communication.

- Outcome: This increased connectivity can strengthen relationships but also create a sense of dependency and over-reliance on digital interaction.

2. Changing Norms and Expectations

- Importance: The digital age has reshaped relationship norms and expectations.

- Outcome: Online interactions and the pace of digital communication influence how relationships progress and what partners expect from each other.

3. Balancing Online and Offline Interactions

- Importance: Maintaining a healthy balance between digital and face-to-face interactions is crucial.

- Outcome: While digital communication is convenient, in-person interactions remain essential for deepening emotional bonds and understanding.

4. Digital Detox and Relationship Health

- Importance: Taking breaks from digital communication can benefit relationship health.

- Outcome: Digital detoxes help couples focus on quality time together, fostering more meaningful connections and reducing the stress of constant connectivity.

The digital age has brought about significant changes in the way we experience and express love. Online dating, social media, and digital communication tools have reshaped romantic relationships, offering both opportunities and challenges. Understanding the impact of technology on love is essential for navigating the complexities of modern relationships. By balancing the advantages of digital connectivity with the importance of genuine, face-to-face interactions, individuals can cultivate healthy, fulfilling relationships in the digital age.

LOVE IN THE DIGITAL AGE: SOCIAL MEDIA

The advent of social media has profoundly transformed the way we connect, communicate, and maintain relationships. While these platforms offer numerous benefits, such as staying in touch with loved ones and sharing life events, they also present unique challenges to romantic relationships. This chapter delves into the influence of social media on relationship dynamics, exploring issues of jealousy, trust, and communication.

The Role of Social Media in Modern Relationships

1. Connecting and Sharing

- Importance: Social media enables couples to stay connected and share their lives more publicly.

- Outcome: Platforms like Facebook, Instagram, and Twitter allow couples to post updates, share photos, and celebrate milestones, fostering a sense of closeness and community.

2. Public Displays of Affection

- Importance: Public displays of affection (PDAs) on social media can reinforce relationship bonds.

- Outcome: Sharing affectionate posts, couple photos, and relationship statuses can validate and affirm the relationship, but may also create pressure to present an idealized image.

3. Maintaining Long-Distance Relationships

- Importance: Social media plays a crucial role in maintaining long-distance relationships.

- Outcome: Video calls, messaging, and social media interactions help bridge the physical gap, providing ways to maintain intimacy and connection despite geographical separation.

Jealousy and Comparison

1. Triggers of Jealousy

- Importance: Social media can trigger jealousy in romantic relationships.

- Outcome: Seeing a partner interact with others online or receiving attention from others can lead to feelings of insecurity and jealousy.

2. Social Comparison

- Importance: Constant exposure to other people's curated lives can lead to unhealthy comparisons.

- Outcome: Comparing one's relationship to the seemingly perfect relationships presented on social media can foster dissatisfaction and self-doubt.

3. Impact on Trust

- Importance: Trust is a foundational element of healthy relationships, which can be strained by social media.

- Outcome: Misunderstandings and assumptions based on social media activity can erode trust, leading to conflicts and doubts about a partner's fidelity and intentions.

Communication in the Age of Social Media

1. Enhanced Communication

- Importance: Social media enhances the frequency and ease of communication.

- Outcome: Couples can communicate more regularly and share their daily lives, strengthening their emotional bond.

2. Miscommunication Risks

- Importance: The absence of nonverbal cues in text-based communication can lead to misinterpretation.

- Outcome: Misunderstandings and miscommunications are common, as tone and intent can be difficult to convey accurately through written messages.

3. Conflict Resolution

- Importance: How couples handle conflicts on social media can impact their relationship health.

- Outcome: Public arguments or passive-aggressive posts can exacerbate conflicts, while private, direct communication is more effective for resolving issues.

Managing Social Media in Relationships

1. Setting Boundaries

- Importance: Establishing boundaries around social media use is essential.

- Outcome: Clear agreements about what is shared online and what remains private can help prevent misunderstandings and protect the relationship's intimacy.

2. Fostering Trust

- Importance: Trust can be fostered by open communication and transparency about social media interactions.

- Outcome: Sharing passwords, being open about online friendships, and discussing social media boundaries can enhance trust and security in the relationship.

3. Healthy Use of Social Media

- Importance: Using social media mindfully can benefit relationships.

- Outcome: Couples who use social media to positively engage with each other and avoid comparisons are likely to experience greater relationship satisfaction.

4. Digital Detox

- Importance: Taking breaks from social media can strengthen relationships.

- Outcome: Regular digital detoxes allow couples to focus on face-to-face interactions, reducing the distractions and pressures associated with constant online connectivity.

Case Studies and Research Findings

1. Research on Social Media and Relationships

- Study Findings: Research indicates that excessive social media use can be linked to higher levels of jealousy and lower relationship satisfaction.

- Implications: Understanding these dynamics can help couples navigate social media use more effectively.

2. Case Study: Social Media and Trust Issues

- Scenario: A couple experiences trust issues due to one partner's frequent interactions with others on social media.

- Resolution: Through open communication and setting clear boundaries, the couple rebuilds trust and strengthens their relationship.

Social media has undeniably reshaped the dynamics of romantic relationships in the digital age. While it offers numerous benefits, such as enhanced communication and connectivity, it also presents challenges, including jealousy, trust issues, and the potential for miscommunication. By understanding the impact of social media on relationships and adopting healthy practices, couples can navigate these challenges and harness the positive aspects of digital connectivity to strengthen their romantic bonds. Through mindful use, clear boundaries, and open communication, love can thrive in the digital age.

LOVE IN THE DIGITAL AGE: LONG DISTANCE RELATIONSHIP

In the digital age, technology has significantly altered the landscape of romantic relationships, particularly for those navigating the complexities of long-distance love. Where once physical distance might have spelled the end for many relationships, today's technology offers myriad tools to bridge the gap. This chapter explores how technology facilitates long-distance relationships, the unique challenges they present, and the opportunities for growth and connection they offer.

The Role of Technology in Long-Distance Relationships

1. Communication Tools

- Importance: Technology provides essential tools for communication in long-distance relationships.

- Outcome: Platforms such as video calls (e.g., Zoom, Skype, FaceTime), instant messaging (e.g., WhatsApp, Messenger), and social media allow couples to stay connected despite physical separation.

2. Video Calls and Virtual Presence

- Importance: Video calls enable face-to-face interaction, which is crucial for maintaining intimacy.

- Outcome: Regular video chats help couples share experiences and maintain a sense of presence, fostering emotional closeness and understanding.

3. Instant Messaging and Social Media

- Importance: Instant messaging and social media provide continuous, real-time communication.

- Outcome: Couples can share their day-to-day lives, send quick updates, and remain involved in each other's routines, which helps sustain the relationship.

4. Shared Digital Activities

- Importance: Engaging in shared digital activities can enhance connection.

- Outcome: Watching movies together through streaming services, playing online games, or participating in virtual events allows couples to create shared experiences, strengthening their bond.

Challenges of Long-Distance Relationships

1. Communication Difficulties

- Importance: Miscommunications can be more frequent in long-distance relationships.

- Outcome: The lack of nonverbal cues and physical presence can lead to misunderstandings and feelings of disconnection.

2. Time Zone Differences

- Importance: Managing different time zones can be challenging.

- Outcome: Coordinating schedules for communication requires extra effort and flexibility, which can strain the relationship.

3. Trust and Insecurity

- Importance: Distance can amplify trust issues and insecurities.

- Outcome: Without regular physical interaction, partners may experience jealousy or fear of infidelity, necessitating strong communication and reassurance.

4. Emotional and Physical Loneliness

- Importance: The absence of physical proximity can lead to feelings of loneliness.

- Outcome: Missing the physical presence and touch of a partner can be emotionally challenging, making it essential to find ways to cope with and address these feelings.

Opportunities for Growth in Long-Distance Relationships

1. Enhanced Communication Skills

- Importance: Long-distance relationships can improve communication skills.

- Outcome: Couples often become more adept at expressing their feelings and resolving conflicts through verbal communication, which can strengthen the relationship overall.

2. Building Trust and Independence

- Importance: Distance requires a higher level of trust and independence.

- Outcome: Partners learn to trust each other deeply and maintain individual lives and activities, which can foster personal growth and resilience.

3. Creative Expressions of Love

- Importance: Distance encourages creativity in expressing love.

- Outcome: Couples often find unique and thoughtful ways to show affection, such as sending surprise gifts, handwritten letters, or planning virtual dates, which can make the relationship more exciting and meaningful.

4. Appreciation and Anticipation

- Importance: Distance can increase appreciation and anticipation for in-person meetings.

- Outcome: The limited physical interaction can make reunions more special and deepen the emotional connection, as partners cherish their time together more.

Strategies for Maintaining a Healthy Long-Distance Relationship

1. Regular and Scheduled Communication

- Strategy: Establishing a regular communication schedule can provide stability and reassurance.

- Outcome: Knowing when they will connect helps partners manage expectations and reduces anxiety about the relationship.

2. Setting Goals and Future Plans

- Strategy: Discussing and planning for the future gives the relationship direction and purpose.

- Outcome: Setting goals for visits, relocations, or future milestones helps couples stay motivated and focused on their long-term commitment.

3. Maintaining Individual Lives

- Strategy: Encouraging each partner to pursue their own interests and social circles.

- Outcome: Maintaining independence ensures that both partners continue to grow individually, which can enhance the relationship's overall health.

4. Practicing Transparency and Honesty

- Strategy: Open and honest communication about feelings, concerns, and expectations.

- Outcome: Transparency builds trust and helps prevent misunderstandings, ensuring both partners feel heard and valued.

5. Using Technology Creatively

- Strategy: Leveraging various digital tools to keep the relationship dynamic.

- Outcome: Exploring new technologies, such as virtual reality for immersive dates or digital photo albums, can keep the relationship fresh and engaging.

Case Studies and Research Findings

1. Research on Long-Distance Relationships

- Study Findings: Studies have shown that long-distance relationships can be as satisfying and stable as geographically close relationships, provided that communication and trust are strong.

- Implications: These findings suggest that with the right tools and mindset, long-distance relationships can thrive.

2. Case Study: Overcoming Time Zone Challenges

- Scenario: A couple navigates a significant time zone difference by establishing a flexible communication schedule and using asynchronous communication methods.

- Resolution: By prioritizing regular updates and being considerate of each other's time, they maintain a strong connection despite the time difference.

Long-distance relationships, once considered untenable by many, have become increasingly feasible in the digital age. Technology offers a wealth of tools to bridge the gap, enabling couples to maintain close and meaningful connections despite physical separation. While long-distance relationships present unique challenges, they also offer opportunities for growth, deeper communication, and creative expressions of love. By leveraging technology wisely and nurturing trust and independence, couples can not only survive but thrive in a long-distance relationship.

CHAPTER 10

PARENTAL LOVE AND ITS PSYCHOLOGICAL EFFECTS

Parental love is a cornerstone of human development, profoundly influencing our emotional and psychological well-being from infancy through adulthood. This form of love is unique in its intensity and impact, providing the foundation for a child's growth, sense of security, and ability to form healthy relationships. In this chapter, we will delve into the nature of parental love and its effects on child development, focusing on attachment and bonding, and how these early experiences shape emotional regulation, social skills, and self-esteem.

Attachment and Bonding

1. Understanding Attachment

- Definition: Attachment refers to the deep emotional bond that develops between a child and their caregiver, typically a parent.

- Significance: This bond is crucial for the child's sense of security and forms the basis for future emotional and social development.

2. John Bowlby's Attachment Theory

- Concept: John Bowlby, the pioneer of attachment theory, proposed that the quality of the early bond between a child and their caregiver significantly affects the child's emotional and psychological development.

- Outcome: Secure attachment leads to healthy emotional regulation and social relationships, while insecure attachment can result in difficulties in these areas.

3. Mary Ainsworth's Strange Situation

- Experiment: Mary Ainsworth expanded on Bowlby's work through the Strange Situation experiment, which identified different attachment styles based on children's reactions to separation and reunion with their caregiver.

- Attachment Styles: Secure, anxious-ambivalent, and avoidant attachment styles, each with distinct patterns of behavior and emotional responses.

4. Impact of Secure Attachment

- Emotional Regulation: Children with secure attachment are better able to manage their emotions and cope with stress.

- Social Skills: These children tend to have more positive social interactions and form healthier relationships.

- Self-Esteem: Secure attachment contributes to higher self-esteem and a stronger sense of self-worth.

5. Impact of Insecure Attachment

- Anxious Attachment: Children with anxious attachment may struggle with clinginess, fear of abandonment, and difficulty managing emotions.

- Avoidant Attachment: These children may exhibit emotional detachment, difficulty with intimacy, and challenges in forming close relationships.

- Long-Term Effects: Insecure attachment can lead to issues such as anxiety, depression, and difficulties in future relationships.

Parental Love and Child Development

1. Emotional Development

- Security and Exploration: A secure attachment provides a safe base from which children can explore their environment, fostering curiosity and learning.

- Emotional Intelligence: Parental love helps children develop emotional intelligence, including empathy, self-awareness, and the ability to understand others' emotions.

2. Cognitive Development

- Brain Development: Positive interactions with loving parents stimulate brain development, enhancing cognitive functions such as problem-solving and language skills.

- Learning and Achievement: Supportive and encouraging parental love promotes a positive attitude towards learning and academic achievement.

3. Social Development

- Social Competence: Children who experience parental love are more likely to develop social competence, including effective communication and conflict resolution skills.

- Peer Relationships: These children tend to have better peer relationships and are more adept at forming and maintaining friendships.

4. Behavioral Outcomes

- Discipline and Boundaries: Parental love provides a framework for discipline, helping children understand boundaries and develop self-control.

- Resilience: Children who feel loved and supported are more resilient, and able to bounce back from setbacks and challenges.

Case Studies and Research Findings

1. Research on Parental Love and Attachment

- Findings: Studies consistently show that secure attachment leads to better emotional and social outcomes, while insecure attachment is linked to various psychological issues.

- Implications: These findings highlight the importance of nurturing and responsive parenting in fostering healthy development.

2. Case Study: The Role of Parental Love in Overcoming Adversity

- Scenario: A child facing significant external challenges, such as poverty or family conflict, shows remarkable resilience and success due to a strong, loving relationship with a parent.

- Analysis: This case illustrates how parental love can provide a crucial buffer against adverse circumstances, supporting the child's emotional and psychological well-being.

Promoting Healthy Attachment and Bonding

1. Responsive Parenting

- Strategy: Being attuned to the child's needs and responding promptly and appropriately.

- Outcome: Fosters secure attachment and helps children feel valued and understood.

2. Consistent Caregiving

- Strategy: Providing consistent and predictable care, including routines and rituals.

- Outcome: Creates a stable environment that supports the child's sense of security and trust.

3. Emotional Availability

- Strategy: Being emotionally present and available, offering comfort and support.

- Outcome: Helps children develop healthy emotional regulation and a strong sense of self.

4. Positive Reinforcement

- Strategy: Using praise and encouragement to reinforce positive behaviors and achievements.

- Outcome: Builds self-esteem and motivates children to pursue their goals and interests.

Parental love is a powerful force that shapes a child's emotional and psychological development in profound ways. Through secure attachment and bonding, children gain the foundation for healthy emotional regulation, social skills, and self-esteem. Understanding the impact of parental love and striving to provide nurturing and responsive care can significantly enhance a child's developmental outcomes. As we continue to explore the complexities of human development, the enduring importance of parental love remains a central and unchanging truth.

THE FOUR PARENTING STYLES

Parental love is not only about the depth of affection a parent has for their child but also how that love is expressed through various parenting styles. Different parenting styles can have significant effects on a child's emotional and psychological development. This chapter will explore the four primary parenting styles—authoritative, authoritarian, permissive, and uninvolved—and their impacts on children's development.

The Four Parenting Styles

1. Authoritative Parenting

- Characteristics: Authoritative parents combine warmth and nurturing with clear boundaries and expectations. They are responsive to their children's needs and encourage independence while maintaining control and guidance.

- Effects on Children: Children of authoritative parents tend to have higher self-esteem, better social skills, and greater psychological resilience. They typically perform well academically and exhibit fewer behavioral problems.

2. Authoritarian Parenting

- Characteristics: Authoritarian parents are highly demanding and controlling, with little warmth or nurturing.

They emphasize obedience and discipline, often through strict rules and harsh punishment.

- Effects on Children: Children raised by authoritarian parents may have lower self-esteem, higher levels of anxiety, and poorer social skills. They may also be more prone to rebellious behavior and have difficulties with authority figures.

3. Permissive Parenting

- Characteristics: Permissive parents are warm and nurturing but provide little structure or discipline. They are indulgent and often allow children to make their own decisions, even if they are not developmentally ready.

- Effects on Children: Children of permissive parents may struggle with self-discipline and authority. They often exhibit impulsive behavior, have poorer academic performance, and may experience difficulties in social settings due to a lack of boundaries.

4. Uninvolved Parenting

- Characteristics: Uninvolved parents are detached and unresponsive, providing minimal warmth or guidance. They are often indifferent to their children's needs and may neglect their emotional and physical well-being.

- Effects on Children: Children with uninvolved parents often experience significant emotional and psychological challenges. They may struggle with self-esteem, exhibit behavioral problems, and have poor social skills and academic performance.

The Impact of Parenting Styles on Child Development

1. Emotional Development

- Authoritative Parenting: Promotes healthy emotional regulation and resilience. Children learn to manage their emotions effectively and develop a positive self-image.

- Authoritarian Parenting: Can lead to emotional suppression and anxiety. Children may struggle with fear of making mistakes and feel less confident in expressing their emotions.

- Permissive Parenting: May result in difficulties with emotional regulation. Children might have trouble coping with frustration and managing their impulses.

- Uninvolved Parenting: Often results in emotional neglect. Children may feel abandoned and unloved, leading to long-term emotional and psychological issues.

2. Social Development

- Authoritative Parenting: Encourages strong social skills and healthy peer relationships. Children learn cooperation, empathy, and effective communication.

- Authoritarian Parenting: Can hinder social development. Children might be overly aggressive or withdrawn and have trouble forming healthy relationships.

- Permissive Parenting: May lead to social challenges. Children might be socially immature and struggle with boundaries in relationships.

- Uninvolved Parenting: Often impairs social skills. Children may have difficulty forming attachments and trusting others.

3. Cognitive Development

- Authoritative Parenting: Supports cognitive growth through encouragement and positive reinforcement. Children are more likely to be curious, motivated, and perform well academically.

- Authoritarian Parenting: Can stifle cognitive development due to fear of failure and lack of encouragement. Children may be less innovative and hesitant to take intellectual risks.

- Permissive Parenting: May not provide enough structure for optimal cognitive development. Children might lack focus and discipline in academic settings.

- Uninvolved Parenting: Neglects cognitive needs. Children may perform poorly academically and show little interest in learning.

4. Behavioral Outcomes

- Authoritative Parenting: Leads to well-adjusted behavior. Children tend to be responsible, self-disciplined, and capable of making good decisions.

- Authoritarian Parenting: May result in either overly compliant or rebellious behavior. Children might follow rules out of fear rather than understanding.

- Permissive Parenting: Often results in impulsive and disobedient behavior. Children might struggle with authority and self-control.

- Uninvolved Parenting: Leads to significant behavioral issues. Children may exhibit defiance, delinquency, and a lack of motivation.

Case Studies and Research Findings

1. Research on Parenting Styles

- Findings: Numerous studies highlight the benefits of authoritative parenting and the drawbacks of the other styles. For instance, research consistently shows that authoritative parenting is associated with the most positive outcomes in children's emotional, social, and cognitive development.

- Implications: These findings emphasize the importance of a balanced approach to parenting that combines warmth with structure and guidance.

2. Case Study: The Effects of Different Parenting Styles in Practice

- Scenario: Comparing the developmental outcomes of three siblings raised with different parenting styles due to changes in family dynamics.

- Analysis: This case illustrates how authoritative parenting promotes healthy development, while authoritarian and permissive styles can lead to various challenges in emotional, social, and academic domains.

Promoting Effective Parenting Practices

1. Balancing Warmth and Control

- Strategy: Combining nurturing behavior with clear expectations and boundaries.

- Outcome: Supports secure attachment, healthy emotional regulation, and positive behavior.

2. Encouraging Independence within Limits

- Strategy: Allowing children to make age-appropriate decisions while providing guidance.

- Outcome: Fosters self-esteem, decision-making skills, and responsibility.

3. Positive Reinforcement

- Strategy: Using praise and rewards to reinforce desirable behavior.

- Outcome: Motivates children and builds confidence.

4. Consistent and Fair Discipline

- Strategy: Applying rules and consequences consistently and fairly.

- Outcome: Helps children understand boundaries and develop self-control.

5. Emotional Support and Communication

- Strategy: Being emotionally available and engaging in open communication.

- Outcome: Enhances emotional intelligence and strengthens the parent-child bond.

Parenting styles profoundly influence children's emotional and psychological development. While authoritative parenting is generally associated with the most positive outcomes, understanding the effects of each style can help parents adapt their approach to better meet their children's needs. By balancing warmth with structure, encouraging independence, and providing consistent support, parents can foster healthy development and build strong, loving relationships with their children. As we continue to explore the complexities of parenting, the importance of thoughtful and responsive parenting practices remains a fundamental truth in nurturing the next generation.

INTERGENERATIONAL RELATIONSHIP

Parental love is a powerful force that significantly shapes a child's emotional and psychological development. This love not only influences the immediate well-being of the child but also has far-reaching effects that extend into adulthood and beyond, shaping future generations. One crucial aspect of this process is the intergenerational transmission of love, where patterns of love and attachment are passed down from one generation to the next. This chapter explores how these patterns develop, their psychological impact, and strategies to foster healthy intergenerational relationships.

Understanding Intergenerational Transmission

1. Definition and Overview

- Intergenerational Transmission: The concept that behaviors, emotions, and attachment patterns are inherited from previous generations. These patterns influence how individuals parent their own children, creating a cycle that can perpetuate both positive and negative traits.

- Mechanisms: This transmission occurs through direct interactions, modeling behaviors, and the emotional climate of the family.

2. The Role of Attachment

- Attachment Theory: According to John Bowlby and Mary Ainsworth, early attachment experiences with caregivers form the foundation for future relationships. Secure, anxious, and avoidant attachment styles can be passed down from parents to children.

- Secure Attachment: Children who experience consistent, responsive, and nurturing care are likely to develop secure attachments and replicate these behaviors with their own children.

- Insecure Attachment: Patterns of anxious or avoidant attachment, often resulting from inconsistent or unresponsive caregiving, can also be transmitted, leading to challenges in future relationships.

Psychological Effects of Intergenerational Transmission

1. Positive Effects

- Healthy Emotional Development: Securely attached individuals often exhibit better emotional regulation, higher self-esteem, and stronger social skills.

- Resilience: Positive patterns of love and attachment can provide a buffer against stress and adversity, fostering resilience in future generations.

- Parenting Practices: Parents who experience secure attachment are more likely to adopt authoritative parenting styles, promoting healthy development in their children.

2. Negative Effects

- Emotional Challenges: Insecure attachment patterns can lead to difficulties in emotional regulation, increased anxiety, and lower self-esteem.

- Relationship Issues: Insecurely attached individuals may struggle with trust, intimacy, and communication in their relationships, perpetuating these issues in their parenting.

- Cycle of Dysfunction: Negative patterns of attachment and love can create a cycle of dysfunction, where each generation replicates the emotional challenges of the previous one.

Factors Influencing Intergenerational Transmission

1. Parental Awareness and Reflection

- Self-Reflection: Parents who reflect on their own attachment experiences and recognize the impact on their parenting are more likely to break negative cycles.

- Therapeutic Interventions: Therapy can help individuals understand and address the patterns of attachment they experienced, promoting healthier relationships with their children.

2. Family Dynamics and Communication

- Open Communication: Families that encourage open and honest communication about emotions and experiences can foster a healthier emotional climate.

- Supportive Environment: A supportive family environment that values emotional expression and nurturance can promote secure attachment across generations.

3. Cultural and Societal Influences

- Cultural Norms: Cultural values and norms around parenting and attachment can shape intergenerational transmission. For example, collectivist cultures may emphasize close family bonds and interdependence, while individualistic cultures may prioritize independence.

- Socioeconomic Factors: Economic stability and access to resources can influence the emotional and psychological well-being of parents, affecting their ability to provide secure attachments.

Case Studies and Research Findings

1. Research on Intergenerational Transmission

- Findings: Studies show that parents who experienced secure attachment are more likely to have children with secure attachment. Conversely, insecure attachment patterns tend to be passed down, highlighting the importance of early intervention and support.

- Implications: These findings underscore the need for policies and programs that support healthy parent-child relationships, such as parenting education and mental health services.

2. Case Study: Breaking the Cycle of Insecure Attachment

- Scenario: A parent who grew up with an avoidant attachment style seeks therapy to address their attachment issues and develop healthier parenting practices.

- Outcome: Through therapy, the parent learns to recognize and modify their behaviors, fostering a secure attachment with their child and breaking the cycle of avoidance.

Strategies to Foster Healthy Intergenerational Relationships

1. Promoting Secure Attachment

- Responsive Parenting: Providing consistent, responsive, and nurturing care to children helps develop a secure attachment and promotes healthy emotional development.

- Emotional Availability: Being emotionally available and attuned to children's needs fosters trust and security.

2. Breaking Negative Cycles

- Therapeutic Support: Accessing therapy to address attachment issues and develop healthier relational patterns can break the cycle of insecure attachment.

- Parenting Education: Programs that educate parents about attachment and effective parenting practices can promote healthier relationships.

3. Building Supportive Communities

- Community Resources: Providing access to resources such as parenting groups, mental health services, and support networks can help families foster secure attachment.

- Cultural Sensitivity: Recognizing and respecting cultural differences in parenting practices can support diverse families in promoting secure attachment.

Parental love and attachment significantly influence children's emotional and psychological development, creating patterns that can be passed down through generations. Understanding the intergenerational transmission of love and attachment helps us recognize the importance of fostering secure relationships and breaking negative cycles. By promoting secure attachment, providing therapeutic support, and building supportive communities, we can ensure healthier emotional and psychological outcomes for future generations. As we continue to explore the complexities of parental love,

the intergenerational transmission of attachment remains a
vital area of focus in nurturing the well-being of children and
families.

117

CHAPTER 11

THE DARK SIDE OF LOVE: JEALOUSY, OBSESSION, AND HEARTBREAK

Love is often celebrated for its capacity to bring joy, fulfillment, and deep connection. However, love can also have a darker side, manifesting in negative emotions and destructive behaviors. This chapter explores the less pleasant aspects of love, including jealousy, obsession, and heartbreak. Understanding these elements is crucial for managing them effectively and fostering healthier, more balanced relationships.

Jealousy in Romantic Relationships

1. Understanding Jealousy

- Definition: Jealousy is an emotional response to a perceived threat to a valued relationship. It often involves feelings of insecurity, fear, and resentment.

- Evolutionary Perspective: From an evolutionary standpoint, jealousy may have developed as a mechanism to protect romantic relationships from external threats, ensuring the survival and well-being of offspring.

2. Causes of Jealousy

- Insecurity and Low Self-Esteem: Individuals with low self-esteem or feelings of inadequacy are more prone to jealousy, fearing that they are not good enough for their partner.

- Past Experiences: Previous experiences of betrayal or infidelity can heighten sensitivity to potential threats, making individuals more susceptible to jealousy.

- Attachment Styles: Those with anxious attachment styles are more likely to experience jealousy due to their fear of abandonment and need for reassurance.

- Perceived Threats: Jealousy can arise from real or imagined threats, such as a partner's close relationship with someone else or attention from a potential rival.

3. Consequences of Jealousy

- Emotional Turmoil: Jealousy can lead to intense emotional distress, including anxiety, anger, and sadness.

- Relationship Strain: Unchecked jealousy can erode trust, communication, and intimacy, leading to conflicts and potential relationship breakdown.

- Destructive Behaviors: In extreme cases, jealousy can result in controlling behaviors, accusations, and even violence.

4. Managing and Overcoming Jealousy

- Self-Reflection: Understanding the root causes of jealousy and addressing underlying insecurities can help mitigate its effects.

- Open Communication: Discussing feelings of jealousy openly and honestly with a partner can foster understanding and reduce misunderstandings.

- Building Trust: Strengthening trust through consistent, reliable behavior and reassurance can help alleviate jealousy.

- Therapeutic Interventions: Therapy can provide tools for managing jealousy, improving self-esteem, and developing healthier relationship patterns.

Obsession in Love

1. Understanding Obsession

- Definition: Obsession in the context of love involves an intense, persistent preoccupation with another person, often to the detriment of one's mental and emotional well-being.

- Difference from Healthy Love: While healthy love is characterized by mutual respect and balance, obsession is often one-sided and can lead to unhealthy attachment and behavior.

2. Causes of Obsession

- Unresolved Emotional Needs: Individuals who have unmet emotional needs or unresolved issues from past relationships may become obsessed with a new partner as a way to fill these voids.

- Attachment Issues: Insecure attachment styles, particularly anxious attachment, can contribute to obsessive behavior.

- Low Self-Worth: People with low self-esteem may become obsessed with a partner who they believe can validate their worth and make them feel complete.

- Idealization: Obsession often involves idealizing the other person, seeing them as perfect and essential for one's happiness.

3. Consequences of Obsession

- Emotional Distress: Obsession can lead to feelings of anxiety, depression, and despair, especially if the feelings are not reciprocated.

- Relationship Imbalance: Obsessive behavior can overwhelm the other person, creating an imbalanced and unhealthy relationship dynamic.

- Impulsive Actions: Obsession can drive individuals to engage in impulsive, irrational, or harmful actions in an attempt to maintain or control the relationship.

4. Managing and Overcoming Obsession

- Self-Awareness: Recognizing obsessive thoughts and behaviors is the first step toward managing them.

- Healthy Boundaries: Establishing and respecting personal boundaries can help prevent obsession from taking over one's life.

- Seeking Support: Therapy and support groups can provide valuable assistance in addressing the underlying issues that contribute to obsession.

- Focusing on Self-Care: Engaging in activities that promote self-esteem and emotional well-being can reduce the intensity of obsessive feelings.

Heartbreak

1. Understanding Heartbreak

- Definition: Heartbreak is the intense emotional pain and distress that follows the end of a significant relationship.

- Physical and Emotional Impact: Heartbreak can manifest physically through symptoms like loss of appetite, sleep disturbances, and fatigue, as well as emotionally through feelings of sadness, anger, and hopelessness.

2. Causes of Heartbreak

- Breakup or Divorce: The end of a romantic relationship, whether through breakup or divorce, is a common cause of heartbreak.

- Unrequited Love: Loving someone who does not reciprocate those feelings can lead to profound emotional pain.

- Betrayal and Infidelity: Discovering a partner's betrayal or infidelity can result in feelings of shock, anger, and profound loss.

3. Consequences of Heartbreak

- Emotional Turmoil: Heartbreak can lead to intense emotional distress, including depression, anxiety, and a sense of emptiness.

- Impact on Self-Esteem: The end of a relationship can challenge one's sense of self-worth and identity.

- Social Isolation: Heartbreak may result in withdrawal from social activities and support networks, exacerbating feelings of loneliness.

4. Healing from Heartbreak

- Allowing Time to Grieve: Acknowledging and allowing oneself to experience the pain of heartbreak is an important step in the healing process.

- Seeking Support: Leaning on friends, family, or a therapist can provide emotional support and perspective during difficult times.

- Focusing on Self-Care: Engaging in activities that promote physical, emotional, and mental well-being can aid in recovery.

- Finding Meaning: Reflecting on the relationship and finding meaning or lessons in the experience can help in moving forward.

Love's darker aspects—jealousy, obsession, and heartbreak—are integral to the human experience of love. By understanding these emotions and behaviors, we can learn to manage them more effectively, fostering healthier and more balanced relationships. While the journey through love's darker sides can be challenging, it also offers opportunities for personal growth, self-awareness, and deeper understanding of oneself and others. Embracing both the light and dark sides of love is essential for cultivating a fulfilling and enduring connection with others.

OBSESSION IN LOVE

While love can be a source of profound joy and fulfillment, it also has a darker side that can manifest in unhealthy ways. One such manifestation is obsession.

Obsessive love is characterized by an overwhelming preoccupation with another person, often to the detriment of one's own well-being and the well-being of the relationship. This chapter delves into the psychological factors that contribute to obsessive love and explores strategies for addressing it through therapy and self-awareness.

Understanding Obsession in Love

1. Definition of Obsessive Love

- Characteristics: Obsessive love is marked by an intense focus on a romantic partner, often accompanied by behaviors such as constant thoughts about the person, excessive need for contact, and difficulty functioning without their presence.

- Difference from Healthy Love: Unlike healthy love, which is balanced and reciprocal, obsessive love is often one-sided and can lead to dependency and controlling behaviors.

2. Psychological Factors Contributing to Obsessive Love

- Attachment Issues: Insecure attachment styles, particularly anxious attachment, can predispose individuals to obsessive behaviors. Those with anxious attachment often fear abandonment and seek constant reassurance, leading to clinginess.

- Low Self-Esteem: Individuals with low self-worth may become obsessed with a partner who they believe can validate their value and provide the affirmation they lack.

- Idealization: Obsession often involves idealizing the other person, seeing them as perfect and essential for one's happiness. This idealization can create unrealistic expectations and dependency.

- Past Trauma: Experiences of trauma, especially related to abandonment or betrayal, can lead to obsessive tendencies as a way to avoid re-experiencing pain.

3. Consequences of Obsessive Love

- Emotional Distress: Obsessive love can lead to significant emotional turmoil, including anxiety, depression, and a sense of emptiness when the partner is not present.

- Relationship Strain: The imbalance created by obsessive behaviors can overwhelm the other person, leading to conflicts, resentment, and potential relationship breakdown.

- Impulsive and Controlling Behaviors: Obsession can drive individuals to engage in controlling or impulsive actions, such as constant checking on the partner, excessive messaging, or even stalking.

Addressing Obsessive Love Through Therapy

1. Therapeutic Approaches

- Cognitive-Behavioral Therapy (CBT): CBT helps individuals identify and challenge irrational thoughts and beliefs that fuel obsessive behaviors. By restructuring these thoughts, individuals can develop healthier patterns of thinking and behavior.

- Attachment-Based Therapy: This approach focuses on understanding and healing attachment issues that contribute to obsessive tendencies. Therapists work with individuals to develop secure attachment patterns and healthier relationship dynamics.

- Mindfulness and Self-Compassion: Mindfulness practices can help individuals become more aware of their obsessive thoughts and behaviors, allowing them to manage these impulses better. Self-compassion exercises can also enhance self-esteem and reduce dependency on external validation.

- Interpersonal Therapy (IPT): IPT addresses the interpersonal issues that contribute to obsessive love, such as communication problems and unresolved conflicts. By improving relational skills, individuals can build more balanced and satisfying relationships.

2. Case Studies and Examples

- Case Study 1: Jane's Story

- Background: Jane struggled with obsessive love after experiencing a traumatic breakup. She constantly checked her ex-partner's social media and felt unable to move on.

- Therapeutic Intervention: Through CBT, Jane learned to challenge her irrational beliefs about needing her ex to feel valued. Mindfulness practices helped her stay present and reduce her compulsive behaviors.

- Outcome: Over time, Jane developed a healthier self-esteem and formed new relationships that were more balanced and fulfilling.

- Case Study 2: Mark's Journey

- Background: Mark had a history of anxious attachment and became obsessed with his new partner, frequently needing reassurance and fearing abandonment.

- Therapeutic Intervention: In attachment-based therapy, Mark explored his early attachment experiences and learned to recognize and address his fears. Techniques from IPT improved his communication skills and helped him express his needs more effectively.

- Outcome: Mark's relationships became more secure and less driven by fear and obsession, leading to a more satisfying romantic connection.

Self-Awareness and Personal Growth

1. Developing Self-Awareness

- Recognizing Obsessive Patterns: Self-awareness involves identifying the thoughts, emotions, and behaviors associated with obsession. Journaling and self-reflection can be valuable tools for this process.

- Understanding Triggers: Identifying the situations or feelings that trigger obsessive behaviors can help individuals manage these impulses more effectively. This might include recognizing patterns related to insecurity or past trauma.

2. Building Healthy Boundaries

- Establishing Personal Boundaries: Setting clear boundaries in relationships is essential for preventing obsessive behaviors. This includes respecting personal space, time, and emotional needs.

- Communicating Boundaries: Open and honest communication with a partner about boundaries can foster mutual respect and understanding, reducing the likelihood of obsession.

3. Fostering Independence and Self-Esteem

- Engaging in Self-Care: Prioritizing self-care activities that promote physical, emotional, and mental well-being can enhance self-esteem and reduce dependency on a partner for validation.

- Pursuing Personal Interests: Engaging in hobbies, social activities, and personal goals can help individuals develop a sense of identity and fulfillment outside of their romantic relationship.

4. Seeking Support

- Therapeutic Support: Professional therapy can provide valuable tools and guidance for addressing obsessive love. Therapists can offer a safe space to explore underlying issues and develop healthier patterns.

- Support Groups: Participating in support groups can provide a sense of community and understanding. Sharing experiences with others facing similar challenges can reduce feelings of isolation and offer practical advice.

Obsessive love, while challenging, is a manageable and treatable condition. By understanding the psychological factors that contribute to obsession and utilizing therapeutic approaches and self-awareness strategies, individuals can develop healthier, more balanced relationships. Recognizing and addressing obsessive tendencies not only enhances personal well-being but also fosters more fulfilling and reciprocal romantic connections. Embracing the journey of personal growth and healing is essential for transforming the darker aspects of love into opportunities for deeper understanding and stronger relationships.

HEARTBREAK

Love, while often a source of immense joy and fulfillment, can also lead to profound pain and suffering when it ends. Heartbreak is a universal experience, characterized by the intense emotional pain that follows the loss of a loved one. Whether through a breakup, divorce, or the death of a partner, heartbreak can feel overwhelming and all-consuming. This chapter explores the emotional and psychological processes involved in coping with grief and moving on from heartbreak.

Understanding Heartbreak

1. The Nature of Heartbreak

- Emotional Pain: Heartbreak is often described as a deep, aching pain in the chest, mirroring the physical sensation of a broken heart. This emotional pain can be as intense as physical pain, affecting one's ability to function.

- Loss and Mourning: Losing a loved one triggers a mourning process similar to grieving a death. This loss can involve not just the person, but also the future plans and dreams that were shared.

2. Stages of Grief

- Denial: Initially, individuals may struggle to accept the reality of the loss, feeling numb or in shock. Denial serves as a defense mechanism to cushion the blow of the emotional pain.

- Anger: As reality sets in, anger may arise, directed at oneself, the former partner, or the circumstances surrounding the loss. This anger can be an outlet for the pain and confusion.

- Bargaining: During this stage, individuals may dwell on "what if" scenarios, hoping to reverse or mitigate the loss. They might make promises or attempt to negotiate with themselves or a higher power.

- Depression: A deep sadness and sense of hopelessness can set in, characterized by withdrawal from social activities, changes in sleep and appetite, and a pervasive sense of despair.

- Acceptance: Over time, individuals begin to accept the reality of the loss, finding ways to move forward and integrate the experience into their lives.

Psychological Processes in Coping with Heartbreak

1. Emotional Regulation

- Acknowledge and Validate Feelings: Recognizing and validating one's emotions is crucial. Allowing oneself to feel the pain, rather than suppressing it, can facilitate healing.

- Expressing Emotions: Finding healthy outlets for emotional expression, such as talking to friends or family, journaling, or engaging in creative activities, can help process feelings.

2. Cognitive Reframing

- Challenging Negative Thoughts: Heartbreak can lead to negative thinking patterns, such as self-blame or hopelessness. Cognitive reframing involves challenging these thoughts and replacing them with more balanced perspectives.

- Finding Meaning: Finding meaning in the experience of loss can help individuals cope. This might involve reflecting on what was learned from the relationship and how it contributed to personal growth.

3. Behavioral Strategies

- Establishing Routines: Maintaining a daily routine can provide structure and a sense of normalcy, helping to navigate the uncertainty and chaos of heartbreak.

- Engaging in Self-Care: Prioritizing self-care activities, such as exercise, proper nutrition, and rest, can support physical and emotional well-being during this challenging time.

4. Social Support

- Seeking Support from Loved Ones: Sharing the burden of grief with trusted friends or family members can provide comfort and reduce feelings of isolation.

- Professional Help: Therapy can offer a safe space to explore and process emotions, develop coping strategies, and navigate the path to healing. Therapists can provide tools for managing grief and rebuilding one's sense of self.

Moving On and Finding Closure

1. Creating New Narratives

- Rewriting the Story: Moving on involves creating new narratives about the relationship and its end. This might include acknowledging both the positive and negative aspects and understanding the role it played in one's life.

- Letting Go of the Past: Finding closure requires letting go of what once was, and embracing the present and future. This might involve symbolic gestures, such as writing a letter to the former partner (without sending it), or participating in a ritual to mark the end of the relationship.

2. Rebuilding Identity and Self-Esteem

- Rediscovering Self: Heartbreak can lead to a loss of identity, especially if one's sense of self was closely tied to the relationship. Rebuilding involves rediscovering personal interests, strengths, and values.

- Strengthening Self-Esteem: Focusing on self-affirmation and self-compassion can help rebuild self-esteem.

This might include setting and achieving personal goals and celebrating small victories.

3. Embracing New Opportunities

- Exploring New Relationships: When ready, opening oneself to new relationships can be a part of healing. This does not necessarily mean romantic relationships; forming new friendships and connections can provide support and enrich one's life.

- Pursuing Passions: Engaging in activities and hobbies that bring joy and fulfillment can provide a sense of purpose and help shift focus away from the pain of the past.

Heartbreak is a deeply painful and transformative experience that affects individuals on multiple levels—emotionally, psychologically, and physically. Understanding the stages of grief and the psychological processes involved in coping with heartbreak can provide a roadmap for navigating this challenging journey. By employing emotional regulation strategies, cognitive reframing, and behavioral approaches, and seeking social support, individuals can find ways to heal and move forward. Ultimately, heartbreak can lead to personal growth and a deeper understanding of oneself, paving the way for healthier and more fulfilling relationships in the future. Embracing the process of healing and rebuilding can transform the pain of heartbreak into an opportunity for renewal and self-discovery.

CHAPTER 12

STRATEGIES FOR NURTURING HEALTHY LOVE RELATIONSHIPS

Building and maintaining a healthy love relationship is an ongoing process that requires dedication, effort, and a willingness to grow together. Successful relationships are characterized by effective communication, mutual respect, trust, and a shared commitment to nurturing the bond. This chapter offers practical strategies for nurturing love relationships, focusing on key areas such as effective communication, conflict resolution, and maintaining emotional intimacy.

Effective Communication

1. Active Listening

   - Presence and Attention: Active listening involves fully focusing on the speaker, making eye contact, and avoiding distractions. This shows respect and validates the speaker's feelings and thoughts.

- Reflective Responses: Paraphrasing or summarizing what the other person has said demonstrates understanding and helps clarify any miscommunications. For example, "What I hear you saying is…"

2. Expressing Feelings and Needs

- Using "I" Statements: Communicating feelings and needs without blaming or criticizing the partner helps reduce defensiveness. For instance, "I feel hurt when…" instead of "You always…"

- Being Honest and Direct: Sharing feelings honestly and directly fosters trust and openness. Avoiding passive-aggressive behavior or bottling up emotions can prevent misunderstandings and resentment.

3. Non-Verbal Communication

- Body Language: Non-verbal cues such as facial expressions, gestures, and posture can significantly impact communication. Being aware of these cues can help convey empathy and understanding.

- Tone of Voice: The tone and pitch of voice can affect how messages are received. A calm, gentle tone can defuse tension, while a harsh or sarcastic tone can escalate conflicts.

Conflict Resolution

1. Identifying the Root Cause

- Underlying Issues: Often, conflicts arise from deeper issues rather than the immediate problem. Identifying these underlying concerns can lead to more meaningful resolutions.

- Patterns of Conflict: Recognizing recurring patterns in conflicts can help address habitual behaviors and find long-term solutions.

2. Staying Calm and Respectful

- Managing Emotions: Taking a break to cool down if emotions are running high can prevent hurtful comments and ensure a more productive discussion.

- Avoiding Blame: Focusing on the issue rather than blaming the partner helps maintain a respectful and collaborative atmosphere.

3. Finding Compromise and Solutions

- Win-Win Solutions: Striving for solutions that satisfy both partners' needs promotes fairness and cooperation. This may involve compromise and flexibility.

- Problem-Solving Approach: Treating conflicts as joint problems to be solved together rather than battles to be won can foster teamwork and mutual support.

Maintaining Emotional Intimacy

1. Quality Time Together

- Shared Activities: Engaging in activities that both partners enjoy can strengthen the bond and create shared experiences.

- Regular Check-Ins: Setting aside time for regular, uninterrupted conversations about each other's feelings, goals, and experiences can maintain emotional closeness.

2. Showing Appreciation and Affection

- Expressing Gratitude: Regularly expressing appreciation for the partner's actions and qualities can enhance feelings of being valued and loved.

- Physical Affection: Non-sexual physical touch, such as hugging, holding hands, or cuddling, can reinforce emotional connection and intimacy.

3. Supporting Each Other's Growth

- Encouraging Individual Interests: Supporting each other's personal interests and goals helps maintain individuality within the relationship and prevents feelings of stagnation.

- Growth Mindset: Viewing the relationship as a dynamic, evolving entity allows both partners to grow together and adapt to changes over time.

Building Trust and Mutual Respect

1. Reliability and Consistency

- Keeping Promises: Consistently following through on commitments builds trust and demonstrates reliability.

- Consistency in Actions: Aligning words with actions reinforces trust and predictability in the relationship.

2. Respecting Boundaries

- Personal Space: Recognizing and respecting each other's need for personal space and autonomy fosters mutual respect.

- Emotional Boundaries: Being mindful of emotional boundaries and not pressuring the partner to share or engage in ways that make them uncomfortable helps maintain respect.

3. Forgiveness and Reconciliation

- Letting Go of Grudges: Holding onto past grievances can erode trust and intimacy. Practicing forgiveness and letting go of grudges is essential for healing and moving forward.

- Constructive Apologies: Offering sincere apologies and taking responsibility for mistakes can facilitate reconciliation and demonstrate a commitment to the relationship.

Enhancing Relationship Satisfaction

1. Shared Goals and Values

- Common Vision: Discussing and aligning on shared goals and values helps create a sense of purpose and direction in the relationship.

- Collaborative Planning: Working together to plan for the future, whether it's setting financial goals, planning trips, or making life decisions, strengthens the partnership.

2. Maintaining Fun and Playfulness

- Humor and Laughter: Incorporating humor and light-heartedness into the relationship can alleviate stress and keep the connection lively and enjoyable.

- Spontaneity: Being open to spontaneous activities and surprises can add excitement and keep the relationship dynamic.

3. Continuous Learning and Improvement

- Relationship Education: Engaging in relationship education, such as reading books, attending workshops, or seeking couples therapy, can provide tools and insights for enhancing the relationship.

- Reflecting on Experiences: Regularly reflecting on the relationship's strengths and areas for improvement can help partners learn and grow together.

Nurturing a healthy love relationship requires continuous effort, effective communication, and a commitment to mutual respect and growth. By employing strategies for improving communication, resolving conflicts constructively, and maintaining emotional intimacy, partners can build a strong, resilient relationship. Trust, appreciation, and support for each other's growth further enhance the connection, creating a fulfilling and enduring bond. Through dedication and a willingness to grow together, couples can navigate the challenges and joys of love, fostering a relationship that brings happiness and enrichment to both partners' lives.

EMOTIONAL

Emotional Intelligence: The Role of Emotional Intelligence in Understanding and Managing Emotions Within Relationships

Emotional intelligence (EI) is a critical factor in fostering healthy love relationships. It involves the ability to recognize, understand, and manage our own emotions, as well as the ability to empathize with the emotions of others. High emotional intelligence can enhance communication, reduce conflict, and deepen emotional connections. This chapter will explore the components of emotional intelligence and offer practical strategies for leveraging EI to nurture and strengthen romantic relationships.

Understanding Emotional Intelligence

1. Components of Emotional Intelligence

- Self-Awareness: Recognizing and understanding one's own emotions, strengths, and weaknesses. This self-knowledge allows individuals to navigate their feelings more effectively.

- Self-Regulation: The ability to manage and control one's emotions, particularly in stressful or challenging situations. This involves staying calm and composed, rather than reacting impulsively.

- Motivation: The drive to achieve goals and maintain a positive attitude, even in the face of setbacks. In relationships, this can translate to a commitment to work through difficulties and sustain a positive dynamic.

- Empathy: The capacity to understand and share the feelings of others. Empathy fosters connection and trust, as it allows individuals to respond compassionately to their partner's needs.

- Social Skills: The ability to manage relationships effectively, communicate clearly, and resolve conflicts constructively. Good social skills enhance collaboration and mutual understanding.

Self-Awareness in Relationships

1. Recognizing Emotional Triggers

- Identifying Patterns: Understanding what situations or behaviors trigger strong emotional reactions can help individuals anticipate and manage their responses.

- Reflective Practices: Journaling, mindfulness, and meditation can help increase self-awareness by providing insight into one's emotional landscape.

2. Understanding Personal Needs and Boundaries

- Articulating Needs: Being clear about one's needs and communicating them effectively can prevent misunderstandings and ensure both partners feel heard and respected.

- Setting Boundaries: Establishing and maintaining healthy boundaries helps protect emotional well-being and fosters respect within the relationship.

Self-Regulation for Healthy Interactions

1. Managing Stress and Emotions

- Relaxation Techniques: Practices such as deep breathing, progressive muscle relaxation, and visualization can help manage stress and maintain emotional balance.

- Pause and Reflect: Taking a moment to pause before responding in emotionally charged situations can prevent reactive behavior and facilitate more thoughtful, constructive interactions.

2. Constructive Expression of Emotions

- I-Statements: Using "I" statements to express feelings without blaming the partner helps communicate emotions in a non-confrontational way.

- Timing and Tact: Choosing the right time and manner to discuss sensitive issues can help ensure that conversations are productive and respectful.

Motivation and Commitment in Relationships

1. Sustaining Positivity

- Positive Reinforcement: Regularly acknowledging and appreciating each other's efforts and qualities can enhance relationship satisfaction and motivation.

- Shared Goals: Setting and working towards shared goals fosters a sense of partnership and mutual support.

2. Overcoming Challenges Together

- Resilience Building: Developing resilience through problem-solving and support can help couples navigate challenges and emerge stronger.

- Growth Mindset: Viewing challenges as opportunities for growth rather than threats can promote a more positive, proactive approach to relationship dynamics.

Empathy and Emotional Connection

1. Active Empathy

- Listening to Understand: Actively listening to understand the partner's perspective, rather than simply waiting for a chance to respond, fosters deeper connection and trust.

- Validation: Acknowledging and validating the partner's feelings, even if one doesn't fully agree with their perspective, helps them feel understood and respected.

2. Expressing Compassion and Support

- Emotional Support: Providing emotional support through empathetic listening and comforting gestures can strengthen the emotional bond.

- Nonverbal Cues: Using nonverbal communication, such as eye contact, touch, and facial expressions, to convey empathy and support.

Social Skills and Relationship Management

1. Effective Communication

- Clear and Honest Expression: Communicating openly and honestly about thoughts and feelings prevents misunderstandings and builds trust.

- Feedback and Reflection: Giving and receiving feedback constructively helps partners grow and improve their relationship dynamics.

2. Conflict Resolution

- Collaborative Problem-Solving: Approaching conflicts as joint problems to be solved together promotes teamwork and mutual respect.

- Compromise and Flexibility: Being willing to compromise and adapt fosters a balanced and harmonious relationship.

Enhancing Emotional Intelligence

1. Personal Development

- Emotional Literacy: Learning to recognize and label emotions accurately can enhance self-awareness and empathy.

- Mindfulness Practices: Mindfulness techniques can help individuals stay present, regulate emotions, and respond more thoughtfully to their partner.

2. Couples' Activities

- Shared Emotional Experiences: Engaging in activities that evoke shared emotional experiences, such as watching movies, attending events, or participating in hobbies, can strengthen the emotional bond.

- Relationship Workshops: Participating in relationship workshops or counseling sessions can provide tools and strategies for enhancing emotional intelligence and relationship skills.

Emotional intelligence plays a vital role in nurturing healthy love relationships. By developing self-awareness, self-regulation, empathy, and social skills, individuals can enhance their ability to understand and manage emotions within the relationship. Effective communication, constructive conflict resolution, and mutual support are key components of emotionally intelligent relationships. Through continuous personal and relational growth, couples can build a resilient, fulfilling, and enduring bond that withstands the challenges of life.

MUTUAL SUPPORT AND RESPECT

Mutual Support and Respect: The Importance of Supporting Each Other's Goals and Aspirations and Respecting Each Other's Individuality

In the landscape of a healthy love relationship, mutual support and respect are foundational pillars that ensure the partnership thrives. Supporting each other's goals and respecting each other's individuality are critical to maintaining a balance between closeness and independence. This chapter delves into how couples can foster an environment of mutual encouragement and respect, highlighting practical strategies for achieving this harmony.

Understanding Mutual Support

1. Encouraging Personal Growth

   - Celebrating Successes: Actively celebrating each other's achievements fosters a sense of partnership and mutual pride. It's essential to acknowledge and rejoice in both big milestones and small victories.

- Providing Emotional Support: Offering a listening ear, empathy, and understanding during challenging times strengthens the emotional bond and demonstrates a commitment to each other's well-being.

2. Supporting Career and Personal Goals

- Goal Setting and Encouragement: Encouraging your partner to pursue their career and personal aspirations involves discussing goals and providing motivation. This support can manifest through verbal encouragement, assistance with planning, or sharing resources.

- Sacrifices and Compromises: Sometimes supporting a partner's goals requires sacrifices, such as adjusting personal schedules or making lifestyle changes. These sacrifices should be made with mutual consent and clear communication to avoid resentment.

Respecting Individuality

1. Maintaining Personal Interests and Hobbies

- Encouraging Autonomy: Respecting each other's need for personal time and space to engage in individual hobbies and interests can prevent feelings of suffocation and dependency. Autonomy within a relationship supports personal identity and satisfaction.

- Shared and Separate Activities: While shared activities can strengthen bonds, having separate interests helps maintain individuality. Balancing both can enrich the relationship by bringing fresh perspectives and experiences.

2. Valuing Differences

- Appreciating Unique Qualities: Recognizing and valuing each other's unique qualities and differences fosters mutual respect. Rather than attempting to change each other, partners should celebrate what makes each person distinct.

- Learning from Each Other: Differences can be opportunities for growth. By being open to learning from each other's experiences and viewpoints, partners can expand their horizons and deepen their connection.

Practical Strategies for Mutual Support and Respect

1. Effective Communication

- Open and Honest Dialogue: Regularly discussing goals, challenges, and feelings ensures both partners are on the same page. Open communication builds trust and prevents misunderstandings.

- Active Listening: Truly listening to your partner's thoughts and concerns without interrupting or judging promotes understanding and empathy. This includes non-verbal cues such as eye contact and nodding.

2. Shared Decision-Making

- Collaborative Planning: Making decisions together about significant aspects of life, such as finances, living arrangements, and future plans, reinforces the sense of partnership. Each person's opinion should be considered and valued.

- Negotiation and Compromise: Finding a middle ground where both partners feel heard and respected is crucial. Compromises should be made with mutual agreement, ensuring that neither partner feels marginalized.

Building a Supportive Environment

1. Creating a Safe Space

- Emotional Safety: Ensuring that both partners feel safe to express their true selves without fear of judgment or rejection is essential. This involves being supportive and non-critical, especially during vulnerable moments.

- Physical Comfort: A comfortable living environment that meets both partners' needs can enhance well-being and relationship satisfaction. This includes respecting personal spaces and boundaries within the home.

2. Encouraging Each Other's Growth

- Continuous Learning: Supporting each other in educational pursuits or personal development activities, such as workshops, courses, or hobbies, fosters a culture of growth and improvement.

- Mentorship and Advice: Acting as a mentor or advisor, when appropriate, can be beneficial. However, it's essential to ensure that advice is given respectfully and without condescension.

Nurturing Respect and Equality

1. Equality in the Relationship

- Balanced Responsibilities: Sharing household chores, financial responsibilities, and other duties equally prevents resentment and promotes fairness. Both partners should feel that their contributions are valued.

- Equal Say in Decisions: Ensuring that both partners have an equal say in decisions affecting the relationship maintains balance and mutual respect. Each person's voice should be heard and considered.

2. Respectful Disagreements

- Healthy Conflict Resolution: Disagreements should be approached with a focus on resolution rather than winning. This involves using "I" statements, staying on topic, and avoiding personal attacks.

- Time-Outs: When conflicts escalate, taking a break to cool down can prevent hurtful exchanges. Agreeing on a time to revisit the discussion can ensure that issues are addressed calmly and constructively.

Fostering Long-Term Mutual Support and Respect

1. Regular Check-Ins

- Scheduled Discussions: Setting aside regular times to discuss the state of the relationship, individual goals, and any concerns helps maintain alignment and address issues promptly.

- Feedback Loops: Providing and receiving constructive feedback about the relationship's dynamics can promote continuous improvement and mutual understanding.

2. Celebrating Together

- Shared Milestones: Celebrating anniversaries, birthdays, and other significant milestones together reinforces the bond and acknowledges the shared journey.

- Spontaneous Gestures: Small, spontaneous acts of kindness and appreciation, such as leaving notes, planning surprise outings, or expressing gratitude, can keep the relationship vibrant and affectionate.

Mutual support and respect are fundamental to nurturing healthy love relationships. By supporting each other's goals and respecting each other's individuality, couples can create a balanced and fulfilling partnership. Effective communication, shared decision-making, and fostering an environment of growth and equality are key strategies to achieve this. Through continuous effort and mutual dedication, partners can build a strong, resilient relationship that thrives on mutual respect and unwavering support.

CHAPTER 13

LOVE BEYOND ROMANTIC RELATIONSHIP

Friendship: The Importance of Friendships in Our Lives and How They Contribute to Our Emotional Well-being

While romantic love often takes the spotlight, other forms of love, such as friendship, familial love, and love for humanity, are equally vital to our emotional and psychological health. Friendships, in particular, play a crucial role in our lives, providing support, companionship, and a sense of belonging. This chapter explores the psychological significance of friendships, their impact on our well-being, and how to cultivate and maintain meaningful friendships.

The Nature of Friendship

1. Definition and Characteristics

- Mutual Affection: Friendships are characterized by mutual affection and emotional bonds between individuals. Unlike romantic relationships, friendships do not typically involve physical intimacy but are rooted in emotional closeness and shared experiences.

- Reciprocity and Equality: Healthy friendships are based on reciprocity and equality, where both parties give and receive support, share responsibilities, and contribute equally to the relationship.

- Trust and Loyalty: Trust and loyalty are foundational to friendships. Friends confide in each other, rely on one another for support, and maintain a sense of loyalty even in challenging times.

2. Types of Friendships

- Acquaintances: These are casual relationships based on shared interests or activities but lacking deeper emotional connection.

- Close Friends: These are individuals with whom we share a significant emotional bond, trust, and regular interaction.

- Best Friends: These are our closest confidants, with whom we share our deepest thoughts, feelings, and experiences. Best friends often occupy a unique and irreplaceable role in our lives.

The Psychological Benefits of Friendship

1. Emotional Support

- Stress Relief: Friends provide a listening ear and emotional support during stressful times, helping to alleviate stress and anxiety. Knowing that someone cares and understands can significantly reduce feelings of isolation and distress.

- Emotional Validation: Friends offer validation of our emotions and experiences, helping us to process and understand our feelings. This emotional validation fosters a sense of acceptance and self-worth.

2. Social Connectedness

- Sense of Belonging: Friendships create a sense of belonging and social connectedness, which is essential for psychological well-being. Being part of a social network provides a feeling of community and reduces feelings of loneliness.

- Identity and Self-Concept: Friends contribute to our identity and self-concept by reflecting our values, interests, and personality traits. Through interactions with friends, we gain insights into ourselves and develop a clearer sense of who we are.

3. Cognitive and Personal Development

- Intellectual Stimulation: Engaging in conversations and activities with friends stimulates intellectual growth and creativity. Friends challenge our thinking, expose us to new ideas, and encourage us to explore different perspectives.

- Personal Growth: Friendships provide opportunities for personal growth and self-improvement.

Friends offer constructive feedback, support our goals, and motivate us to pursue our aspirations.

Cultivating and Maintaining Friendships

1. Building Friendships

- Common Interests: Friendships often form around shared interests, hobbies, and activities. Participating in social events, clubs, or groups related to your interests can help you meet like-minded individuals.

- Initiating Contact: Taking the initiative to reach out and express interest in getting to know someone better is crucial. Simple gestures like inviting someone for coffee or a walk can be the starting point of a meaningful friendship.

2. Maintaining Friendships

- Regular Communication: Staying in touch and regularly communicating with friends is essential for maintaining strong connections. This can include phone calls, text messages, social media interactions, or face-to-face meetings.

- Quality Time: Spending quality time together strengthens the bond between friends. Engaging in shared activities, creating new memories, and being present in each other's lives are vital components of lasting friendships.

- Support and Empathy: Offering support and empathy during both good times and bad is crucial for maintaining friendships. Being there for your friends, listening to their concerns, and offering help when needed reinforces trust and loyalty.

Challenges in Friendships

1. Conflict and Resolution

- Misunderstandings and Disagreements: Conflicts and disagreements are natural in any relationship. Addressing issues openly, with respect and a willingness to understand the other person's perspective, is key to resolving conflicts.

- Forgiveness and Reconciliation: Practicing forgiveness and working towards reconciliation after conflicts can strengthen friendships. Holding onto grudges can damage the relationship, whereas forgiveness fosters healing and growth.

2. Changes in Life Circumstances

- Life Transitions: Major life changes, such as moving, changing jobs, or starting a family, can impact friendships. Being adaptable and finding new ways to stay connected can help maintain the relationship through these transitions.

- Evolving Dynamics: As individuals grow and change, so do their friendships. Being open to evolving dynamics and adjusting expectations can help sustain long-term friendships.

Friendships are an integral part of our lives, contributing significantly to our emotional well-being, personal growth, and overall happiness. By understanding the nature and importance of friendships, we can cultivate and maintain meaningful connections that enrich our lives. Through mutual support, regular communication, and a willingness to navigate challenges together, friendships can become a lasting source of joy, comfort, and fulfillment. In the broader spectrum of love, friendships remind us that love transcends romantic relationships, encompassing a wide range of deep, meaningful connections that shape our lives and identities.

FAMILY LOVE

Familial Love: The Bonds Between Family Members and Their Impact on Our Psychological Health

Familial love, the deep bonds between family members, is a fundamental aspect of human experience that profoundly impacts our psychological health and development. This chapter explores the nature of familial love, its various forms, and the significant influence it has on our emotional and psychological well-being.

The Nature of Familial Love

1. Definition and Characteristics

- Unconditional Love: Familial love is often characterized by its unconditional nature, where family members support and care for each other regardless of circumstances. This unconditional love provides a sense of security and acceptance.

- Shared History and Experiences: Family members share a unique history and set of experiences that contribute to strong emotional bonds. These shared memories and traditions create a sense of continuity and belonging.

- Interdependence: Familial relationships are marked by interdependence, where members rely on each other for emotional, social, and sometimes financial support. This mutual reliance fosters close-knit connections.

2. Types of Familial Love

- Parental Love: The love between parents and their children is foundational, providing the initial context for a child's emotional and psychological development. Parental love involves nurturing, protection, and guidance.

- Sibling Love: Relationships between siblings can be some of the longest-lasting in a person's life. Sibling love often includes companionship, rivalry, and mutual support.

- Extended Family: Relationships with grandparents, aunts, uncles, and cousins also contribute to a person's support network. These relationships often provide additional sources of love, wisdom, and guidance.

The Psychological Benefits of Familial Love

1. Emotional Support

- Stress Relief: Family members often provide a primary source of emotional support during stressful times. Knowing that one has a reliable support system can significantly reduce stress and anxiety.

- Emotional Validation: Family can offer validation and understanding, helping individuals to process and make sense of their emotions. This validation fosters self-esteem and emotional resilience.

2. Socialization and Identity Formation

- Social Skills: Family interactions are the first context in which individuals learn social skills, such as communication, conflict resolution, and empathy. These skills are critical for forming healthy relationships outside the family.

- Identity and Self-Concept: Family influences our sense of identity and self-concept. The values, beliefs, and traditions passed down through family shape our understanding of who we are and our place in the world.

3. Security and Stability

- Attachment and Bonding: Secure attachments with family members, particularly during childhood, provide a foundation for healthy relationships later in life. These bonds create a sense of stability and trust.

- Predictability and Routine: Family life often provides structure and routine, which can contribute to a sense of security and predictability. This stability is especially important for children's development.

Challenges in Familial Relationships

1. Conflict and Resolution

- Generational Differences: Differences in values and perspectives between generations can lead to conflicts. Effective communication and mutual respect are key to navigating these differences.

- Rivalry and Jealousy: Sibling rivalry and jealousy can strain relationships. Addressing these issues openly and fostering a culture of support and fairness can mitigate these tensions.

2. Life Transitions

- Changes in Family Structure: Life events such as divorce, remarriage, or the death of a family member can significantly impact familial relationships. Coping with these changes requires adaptability and support.

- Aging and Caregiving: As family members age, roles often shift, with younger members taking on caregiving responsibilities. This can create new dynamics and challenges that require compassion and cooperation.

3. Toxic Family Dynamics

- Abuse and Neglect: In some families, relationships can be harmful, involving abuse or neglect. Recognizing these toxic dynamics and seeking external support or intervention is crucial for the well-being of affected individuals.

- Enmeshment: Overly close family relationships, where boundaries are blurred, can hinder individual autonomy and personal growth. Establishing healthy boundaries is essential for maintaining balanced relationships.

Strengthening Familial Bonds

1. Effective Communication

- Open Dialogue: Encouraging open and honest communication within the family helps to resolve conflicts and strengthen bonds. Listening actively and expressing feelings constructively are key components of effective communication.

- Family Meetings: Regular family meetings can provide a platform for discussing issues, planning activities, and making decisions collaboratively. This practice fosters a sense of unity and shared responsibility.

2. Quality Time

- Shared Activities: Engaging in shared activities, such as family dinners, vacations, or hobbies, helps to build positive memories and strengthen connections. These activities provide opportunities for bonding and enjoyment.

- Traditions and Rituals: Family traditions and rituals, whether related to holidays, birthdays, or other special occasions, contribute to a sense of continuity and identity. These practices reinforce family bonds and create lasting memories.

3. Supportive Environment

- Encouragement and Praise: Offering encouragement and praise for achievements and efforts fosters a positive and supportive environment. Recognizing each family member's strengths and contributions enhances self-esteem and mutual respect.

- Emotional Availability: Being emotionally available and responsive to each other's needs strengthens familial bonds. This availability demonstrates care and concern, reinforcing the sense of security and support.

Familial love is a cornerstone of our emotional and psychological well-being, providing essential support, stability, and a sense of belonging. By understanding the nature and importance of familial love, we can cultivate and maintain healthy, supportive relationships that enrich our lives. Navigating challenges, fostering open communication, and spending quality time together are key strategies for strengthening familial bonds. Ultimately, the love we experience within our families shapes our identities, influences our relationships, and contributes to our overall happiness and fulfillment.

ALTRUISTIC LOVE

Altruistic Love: The Concept of Love for Humanity and How Acts of Kindness and Compassion Can Enhance Our Sense of Purpose and Fulfillment

Altruistic love, or love for humanity, transcends personal relationships and encompasses a broader sense of compassion, kindness, and selflessness toward others. This form of love, often associated with acts of charity, volunteerism, and social justice, reflects a deep concern for the well-being of others. In this chapter, we will explore the concept of altruistic love, its psychological underpinnings, and how engaging in acts of kindness and compassion can enhance our sense of purpose and fulfillment.

Understanding Altruistic Love

1. Definition and Characteristics

- Selflessness: Altruistic love involves selfless concern for the welfare of others, without expecting anything in return. It is characterized by genuine empathy and a desire to help those in need.

- Universal Compassion: This form of love extends beyond personal connections to include strangers and humanity as a whole. It reflects a deep sense of empathy and compassion for all living beings.

- Moral and Ethical Dimension: Altruistic love is often driven by moral and ethical principles, including a sense of justice, fairness, and responsibility to contribute positively to society.

2. The Roots of Altruistic Love

- Evolutionary Perspective: From an evolutionary standpoint, altruistic behavior can enhance group survival and cohesion. Acts of kindness and cooperation within communities have historically contributed to collective well-being.

- Cultural and Religious Influences: Many cultures and religions emphasize the importance of altruism and compassion. Teachings from various traditions encourage individuals to practice kindness, generosity, and selflessness.

- Psychological Foundations: Psychological theories suggest that altruistic love is rooted in empathy and the ability to understand and share the feelings of others. Mirror neurons and social learning play a role in fostering empathetic responses.

The Psychological Benefits of Altruistic Love

1. Enhanced Sense of Purpose

- Meaningful Engagement: Engaging in acts of kindness and helping others provides a sense of purpose and fulfillment. It allows individuals to feel that their actions contribute to a greater good.

- Positive Impact: Knowing that one's efforts can make a difference in the lives of others enhances a sense of meaning and significance. This awareness fosters a deeper connection to humanity and a sense of shared responsibility.

2. Improved Mental Health

- Reduced Stress and Anxiety: Altruistic behavior has been linked to reduced levels of stress and anxiety. Helping others can provide a sense of control and accomplishment, counteracting feelings of helplessness.

- Increased Happiness and Well-Being: Acts of kindness trigger the release of endorphins, often referred to as the "helper's high." This neurochemical response contributes to increased happiness and overall well-being.

- Social Connection: Altruistic actions strengthen social bonds and create a sense of community. These connections provide emotional support and reduce feelings of isolation and loneliness.

3. Personal Growth and Self-Esteem

- Empathy and Compassion: Practicing altruistic love enhances empathy and compassion, leading to personal growth and emotional intelligence. It allows individuals to develop a deeper understanding of others' experiences and perspectives.

- Self-Worth: Contributing to the well-being of others boosts self-esteem and self-worth. Knowing that one's actions are valuable and appreciated reinforces a positive self-concept.

Cultivating Altruistic Love

1. Everyday Acts of Kindness

- Small Gestures: Simple acts of kindness, such as smiling at a stranger, holding the door open, or offering a compliment, can have a significant positive impact. These small gestures contribute to a culture of kindness and compassion.

- Volunteering: Dedicating time to volunteer for charitable organizations or community projects is a powerful way to practice altruistic love. Volunteering provides opportunities to make a tangible difference in the lives of others.

- Random Acts of Kindness: Engaging in random acts of kindness, such as paying for someone's coffee or leaving a kind note, can create ripple effects of positivity and inspire others to do the same.

2. Supporting Social Causes

- Advocacy and Activism: Supporting social causes and advocating for justice, equality, and human rights are expressions of altruistic love. Participating in activism and raising awareness about important issues can drive positive social change.

- Donations and Charity: Contributing financially to charitable organizations and causes is another way to practice altruistic love. Donations can support initiatives that address poverty, education, healthcare, and other critical needs.

3. Fostering Empathy and Compassion

- Mindfulness and Reflection: Practicing mindfulness and reflecting on one's actions and motivations can deepen empathy and compassion. Understanding the impact of one's behavior on others fosters a more altruistic mindset.

- Education and Awareness: Learning about the challenges and struggles faced by different communities and individuals can enhance empathy and compassion. Education encourages informed and compassionate responses to societal issues.

The Ripple Effect of Altruistic Love

1. Spreading Positivity

- Inspiration and Influence: Acts of altruistic love can inspire others to engage in similar behavior. Witnessing kindness and compassion often motivates individuals to adopt these practices in their own lives.

- Creating a Culture of Compassion: When individuals consistently practice altruistic love, they contribute to creating a culture of compassion and empathy within their communities. This culture promotes collective well-being and social harmony.

2. Long-Term Impact

- Sustainable Change: Altruistic actions can lead to sustainable social and environmental change. Efforts to address systemic issues, such as poverty, inequality, and environmental degradation, have long-lasting positive effects on society.

- Legacy of Love: The impact of altruistic love extends beyond the immediate effects of individual actions. It creates a legacy of compassion and kindness that can be passed down through generations, fostering a more compassionate and just world.

Altruistic love, or love for humanity, is a powerful force that transcends personal relationships and contributes to our sense of purpose, fulfillment, and psychological well-being. By understanding the nature of altruistic love and actively engaging in acts of kindness and compassion, we can enhance our own lives and positively impact the lives of others. Cultivating altruistic love involves everyday acts of kindness, supporting social causes, and fostering empathy and compassion. The ripple effect of altruistic love creates a culture of compassion and drives sustainable positive change, leaving a legacy of love that benefits humanity as a whole.

CHAPTER 14

THE FUTURE OF LOVE: TRENDS AND PREDICTIONS

The Impact of AI and Robotics: The Potential for Artificial Intelligence and Robots to Influence Romantic Relationships and Companionships

The nature of love and relationships is continually evolving, influenced by advances in technology, shifting cultural norms, and changing societal expectations. As we move further into the 21st century, the role of artificial intelligence (AI) and robotics in shaping romantic relationships and companionship becomes increasingly significant. This chapter explores the potential impact of AI and robotics on love, examining both the opportunities and challenges that these technological advancements present.

AI and Robotics in Romantic Relationships

1. AI-Enhanced Matchmaking

- Algorithmic Matching: Dating apps and websites have long utilized algorithms to match individuals based on compatibility factors. However, advancements in AI are making these algorithms more sophisticated, incorporating machine learning to predict compatibility with greater accuracy.

- Personalization: AI can analyze vast amounts of data to provide personalized recommendations for potential partners. This level of personalization can enhance the user experience and increase the likelihood of finding a compatible match.

2. Virtual Companions

- AI Chatbots: AI chatbots, designed to simulate human conversation, are becoming increasingly sophisticated. These virtual companions can provide emotional support, and companionship, and even simulate aspects of romantic relationships.

- Emotional AI: Advances in emotional AI allow virtual companions to recognize and respond to human emotions. This capability enhances the sense of connection and emotional intimacy between humans and AI companions.

3. Robotic Companions

- Social Robots: Social robots, equipped with AI, are designed to interact with humans in meaningful ways. These robots can engage in conversations, provide companionship, and even simulate romantic behaviors.

- Physical Affection: Some robotic companions are designed to mimic physical affection, such as hugging or holding hands. These features can provide comfort and a sense of closeness to individuals who may be lonely or isolated.

Opportunities and Benefits

1. Addressing Loneliness and Isolation

- Companionship for the Lonely: AI and robotic companions can provide companionship to individuals who are lonely or socially isolated. This can be particularly beneficial for the elderly, individuals with disabilities, or those living alone.

- Emotional Support: Virtual and robotic companions can offer emotional support and empathy, helping individuals cope with stress, anxiety, and other emotional challenges.

2. Enhancing Relationship Skills

- Practice and Feedback: AI companions can provide a safe environment for individuals to practice social and relationship skills. Feedback from AI can help users improve their communication and emotional intelligence.

- Therapeutic Applications: AI and robotic companions can be used in therapeutic settings to help individuals work through relationship issues or develop healthier relationship patterns.

3. Customization and Personalization

- Tailored Interactions: AI companions can be customized to meet the specific needs and preferences of individuals. This level of personalization can enhance the user experience and provide more meaningful interactions.

- Adaptive Learning: AI systems can learn and adapt over time, becoming more attuned to the preferences and behaviors of their human counterparts. This adaptability can create a more engaging and dynamic relationship.

Challenges and Ethical Considerations

1. Emotional Dependence

- Over-Reliance on AI: There is a risk that individuals may become overly dependent on AI companions, leading to reduced social interactions with humans. This dependency could impact the development of real-life social and relationship skills.

- Attachment and Disconnection: Emotional attachment to AI companions can create a disconnection from real human relationships. It is important to balance the benefits of AI companionship with maintaining healthy human connections.

2. Privacy and Data Security

- Data Collection: AI companions often require access to personal data to function effectively. Ensuring the privacy and security of this data is crucial to prevent misuse or unauthorized access.

- Ethical Use of Data: The ethical use of data collected by AI companions is a significant concern. Clear guidelines and regulations are needed to protect user privacy and ensure that data is used responsibly.

3. Societal Impact

- Changing Relationship Norms: The integration of AI and robotic companions into society could alter traditional relationship norms and expectations. This shift may lead to changes in how relationships are perceived and valued.

- Economic and Social Inequality: Access to advanced AI and robotic companions may be limited by economic and social factors. Ensuring equitable access to these technologies is important to prevent further inequalities.

The Future of Human-AI Relationships

1. Hybrid Relationships

- Integration with Human Relationships: AI and robotic companions can complement human relationships rather than replace them. Hybrid relationships, where AI enhances human connections, may become more common.

- Support for Caregivers: AI companions can provide support to caregivers, easing the burden of care and allowing for more meaningful interactions with loved ones.

2. Evolving AI Capabilities

- Continual Advancements: The capabilities of AI and robotic companions will continue to evolve, becoming more sophisticated and human-like. This evolution will enhance their ability to provide meaningful companionship and support.

- Ethical AI Development: Ensuring that AI development prioritizes ethical considerations and human well-being will be crucial. Transparent and responsible AI practices will help build trust and acceptance.

3. Societal Acceptance

- Cultural Adaptation: As AI and robotic companions become more integrated into society, cultural adaptation and acceptance will play a key role in their success. Public perception and societal norms will influence the adoption and use of these technologies.

- Policy and Regulation: Developing policies and regulations that address the ethical, legal, and social implications of AI and robotic companions will be essential. These frameworks will help guide the responsible use of technology in relationships.

The future of love and relationships is poised for significant transformation with the advent of AI and robotics. These technologies offer exciting opportunities for enhancing companionship, addressing loneliness, and improving relationship skills. However, they also present challenges and ethical considerations that must be carefully navigated. As AI and robotic companions become more integrated into our lives, it is essential to balance the benefits of technology with the importance of maintaining genuine human connections. By embracing the potential of AI while prioritizing ethical and responsible practices, we can create a future where love and relationships are enriched by technology, fostering deeper connections and greater well-being.

CHANGING SOCIAL NORMS

Changing Social Norms: How Shifting Attitudes Toward Marriage, Gender Roles, and Family Structures Are Reshaping the Landscape of Love

The concept of love and relationships is evolving in response to changing social norms and cultural shifts. These transformations are reshaping how we perceive marriage, gender roles, and family structures. This chapter explores the impact of these shifting attitudes on the landscape of love, examining how contemporary societal changes influence our relationships and expectations.

The Evolution of Marriage

1. Declining Marriage Rates

- Changing Priorities: As societal priorities shift, many individuals are choosing to delay or forgo marriage. Career aspirations, personal development, and financial stability are often prioritized over traditional timelines for marriage.

- Alternative Relationships: Increasingly, people are exploring alternative forms of relationships such as cohabitation, domestic partnerships, and open relationships, challenging the traditional notion of marriage.

2. Marriage Redefined

- Same-Sex Marriage: The legalization of same-sex marriage in many parts of the world has redefined the traditional concept of marriage, promoting inclusivity and equality in romantic partnerships.

- Cultural Diversity: Cross-cultural marriages are becoming more common, bringing together diverse traditions and practices. This cultural exchange enriches the institution of marriage, fostering greater understanding and acceptance.

3. The Rise of Singlehood

- Empowerment and Independence: There is a growing acceptance of singlehood as a valid and fulfilling life choice. Single individuals are embracing independence, self-sufficiency, and personal freedom, challenging the societal expectation that marriage is necessary for happiness.

- Support Networks: Strong social networks and communities provide emotional support for single individuals, reducing the stigma associated with being unmarried.

Shifting Gender Roles

1. Gender Equality in Relationships

- Shared Responsibilities: Modern relationships are increasingly characterized by shared responsibilities in household chores, child-rearing, and financial support. This shift promotes equality and mutual respect between partners.

- Dual-Career Couples: The rise of dual-career couples has changed the dynamics of relationships, with both partners pursuing professional ambitions. Balancing career and family life requires cooperation and flexibility.

2. Breaking Stereotypes

- Non-Traditional Roles: Traditional gender roles are being challenged, with men and women taking on roles that were once considered unconventional. Stay-at-home dads and career-oriented women are becoming more common, breaking down gender stereotypes.

- Fluidity and Flexibility: Gender identity and expression are increasingly recognized as fluid and diverse. This flexibility allows individuals to define their roles and relationships in ways that feel authentic and fulfilling.

3. Impact on Intimacy and Communication

- Emotional Expression: Evolving gender roles encourage open emotional expression and vulnerability, enhancing intimacy and communication in relationships. Men, in particular, are finding greater acceptance in expressing their emotions.

- Negotiation and Adaptation: Couples are learning to negotiate and adapt to changing roles and expectations, fostering a more dynamic and resilient partnership.

Redefining Family Structures

1. Blended Families

- Complex Dynamics: Blended families, formed through remarriage or cohabitation, present unique dynamics and challenges. Navigating relationships with step-parents, step-siblings, and extended family requires communication and empathy.

- Support Systems: Building strong support systems and establishing clear boundaries can help blended families thrive, fostering a sense of belonging and stability.

2. Chosen Families

- Community and Friendship: Chosen families, composed of close friends and community members, provide emotional support and companionship. These non-traditional family structures challenge the notion that biological ties are the only basis for family.

- Inclusivity and Acceptance: Chosen families promote inclusivity and acceptance, offering a sense of belonging to individuals who may feel disconnected from their biological families.

3. Single-Parent and Co-Parenting

- Single-Parent Households: Single-parent households are becoming more common, with individuals successfully raising children on their own. This shift challenges the traditional family model and highlights the strength and resilience of single parents.

- Co-Parenting Arrangements: Co-parenting arrangements, where separated or divorced parents share custody and responsibilities, emphasize collaboration and the well-being of the children. Effective co-parenting requires communication and cooperation.

The Impact on Romantic Relationships

1. Increased Autonomy and Independence

- Personal Growth: Shifting social norms encourage individuals to prioritize personal growth and self-fulfillment.

This focus on individual development enhances the quality of romantic relationships, as partners bring their best selves to the partnership.

- Interdependence: Healthy relationships balance autonomy and interdependence, allowing partners to support each other while maintaining their individuality.

2. Evolving Expectations

- Redefining Success: Success in relationships is increasingly defined by mutual happiness, personal growth, and emotional connection rather than traditional milestones like marriage and children.

- Flexible Commitment: Modern relationships embrace flexibility in commitment, recognizing that each partnership is unique. This flexibility allows couples to define their own terms and navigate changes together.

3. Technology and Connectivity

- Digital Communication: Technology facilitates constant communication and connectivity, allowing couples to maintain closeness despite physical distance. Video calls, messaging apps, and social media enhance long-distance relationships.

- Online Communities: Online communities and support groups provide valuable resources and connections for individuals navigating non-traditional relationships, offering guidance and shared experiences.

The landscape of love is continually evolving in response to changing social norms, cultural shifts, and technological advancements. As attitudes toward marriage, gender roles, and family structures transform, so too do our romantic relationships and expectations. Embracing these changes requires flexibility, open-mindedness, and a willingness to redefine traditional notions of love and partnership. By understanding and adapting to these evolving dynamics, we can foster deeper, more meaningful connections and create a future where love is inclusive, diverse, and empowering.

THE ROLE OF TECHNOLOGY: INNOVATIONS IN COMMUNICATION AND VIRTUAL REALITY

As we progress further into the digital age, technology continues to revolutionize various aspects of our lives, including how we experience love and maintain relationships. Innovations in communication and virtual reality are at the forefront of this transformation, offering new ways to connect, interact, and sustain emotional bonds. This chapter delves into the role of technology in shaping the future of love, examining its potential to enhance and challenge traditional relationship dynamics.

Innovations in Communication

1. Instant Connectivity

- Messaging Apps: Platforms like WhatsApp, Messenger, and Telegram enable instant communication, allowing couples to stay connected regardless of physical distance. These apps support text, voice, and video messaging, fostering continuous engagement.

- Social Media: Social media platforms such as Facebook, Instagram, and Twitter provide avenues for sharing experiences, expressing emotions, and staying updated on each other's lives. They also offer public affirmation of relationships through posts, likes, and comments.

2. Video Communication

- Video Calls: Video calling services like Skype, Zoom, and FaceTime bridge geographical gaps, allowing for face-to-face interaction. This technology is particularly beneficial for long-distance relationships, helping partners maintain visual and emotional intimacy.

- Virtual Dates: Couples can engage in virtual dates using video communication, participating in activities like cooking together, watching movies, or playing online games. This creates shared experiences and strengthens emotional connections.

3. AI-Powered Communication

- Chatbots and Virtual Assistants: AI-driven chatbots and virtual assistants can facilitate relationship management by sending reminders for anniversaries, suggesting date ideas, and even mediating conflicts through guided conversations.

- Language Translation: Real-time language translation apps break down language barriers in international relationships, enabling partners to communicate more effectively and understand each other's cultural contexts.

Virtual Reality and Augmented Reality

1. Virtual Reality (VR)

- Immersive Experiences: VR technology offers immersive experiences that can simulate physical presence. Couples can use VR headsets to explore virtual environments together, from scenic landscapes to interactive games, enhancing their bond through shared adventures.

- Virtual Touch: Innovations in haptic technology allow users to experience a sense of touch in virtual environments. This can be particularly meaningful in long-distance relationships, providing a semblance of physical closeness and intimacy.

2. Augmented Reality (AR)

- Enhanced Communication: AR applications overlay digital information onto the real world, enriching communication with visual and contextual elements. For example, couples can leave virtual notes and reminders for each other in their living spaces.

- Interactive Experiences: AR can create interactive experiences that blend the virtual and physical worlds. Couples can engage in activities like virtual scavenger hunts, enhancing their relationship through playful interaction.

The Impact on Relationship Dynamics

1. Increased Accessibility and Flexibility

- Global Connections: Technology enables individuals to form relationships across the globe, transcending geographical limitations. This increases the diversity of relationships and broadens the potential for finding compatible partners.

- Flexible Communication: The flexibility of digital communication allows couples to interact at their convenience, accommodating different time zones and schedules. This adaptability supports the maintenance of relationships in a fast-paced world.

2. Challenges of Digital Relationships

- Miscommunication: Despite the advantages of instant communication, digital interactions can sometimes lead to misunderstandings due to the lack of non-verbal cues. Emojis and text-based communication may not fully convey tone and intent.

- Digital Overload: The constant connectivity facilitated by technology can lead to digital overload, causing stress and reducing the quality of interactions. Couples must navigate the balance between online and offline engagement to maintain a healthy relationship.

3. Privacy and Security

- Data Protection: As technology becomes more integrated into relationships, the importance of data privacy and security increases. Couples must be aware of the risks associated with sharing personal information online and take steps to protect their digital privacy.

- Cybersecurity: Ensuring the security of communication platforms is crucial to prevent breaches and unauthorized access. Strong passwords, encryption, and secure networks are essential for safeguarding intimate interactions.

Future Trends and Predictions

1. AI and Machine Learning

- Personalized Relationship Coaching: AI-driven relationship coaching services can offer personalized advice and support based on analysis of communication patterns and behaviors. This technology can help couples navigate challenges and enhance their relationship skills.

- Emotion Recognition: Advanced AI algorithms can analyze facial expressions, voice tones, and text to recognize emotions, providing insights into each partner's emotional state. This can facilitate deeper understanding and empathy in relationships.

2. Virtual Companions

- AI Companions: The development of AI companions, or virtual partners, raises intriguing possibilities and ethical questions. These companions can provide emotional support and companionship, potentially complementing or complicating human relationships.

- Human-Robot Relationships: As robotics technology advances, the potential for human-robot relationships emerges. These relationships challenge traditional notions of love and companionship, prompting discussions about the nature of intimacy and connection.

3. Enhanced Reality Integration

- Mixed Reality Experiences: The integration of augmented and virtual reality with the physical world creates mixed reality experiences that can enrich relationships. Couples can seamlessly blend digital and real-world interactions, fostering creativity and innovation in their connection.

- Telepresence: Telepresence technology, which allows users to project themselves into remote locations using advanced robotics and VR, can revolutionize long-distance relationships. Partners can experience a sense of presence and interaction that transcends current limitations.

The role of technology in shaping the future of love is profound and multifaceted. Innovations in communication and virtual reality are transforming how we connect, interact, and maintain relationships. While these advancements offer exciting opportunities for enhancing intimacy and overcoming physical barriers, they also present challenges that require careful navigation. As we embrace the possibilities of a digitally connected world, understanding the impact of technology on love and relationships will be crucial for fostering meaningful and fulfilling connections. The future of love lies at the intersection of human emotions and technological innovation, promising a landscape rich with potential and complexity.

CONCLUSION

THE POWER AND COMPLEXITY OF LOVE

Love is a multifaceted phenomenon that encompasses an array of emotions, behaviors, and psychological states. As we conclude our exploration of the psychology of love, it is essential to reflect on the insights gained throughout this journey and acknowledge the enduring mystery that love presents. From the neurobiological underpinnings and psychological theories to the impact of technology and cultural variations, our understanding of love continues to evolve. Despite its complexities, love remains a fundamental aspect of the human experience, profoundly influencing our lives and relationships.

The Dual Nature of Love

1. Immense Joy and Fulfillment

- Emotional Bonding: Love fosters deep emotional connections, creating bonds that provide comfort, security, and a sense of belonging. These bonds are the foundation of healthy relationships, promoting mutual support and personal growth.

- Life Satisfaction: Engaging in loving relationships enhances life satisfaction and overall well-being. The positive emotions associated with love, such as happiness, contentment, and joy, contribute to a fulfilling life.

2. Deep Pain and Suffering

- Heartbreak: The loss of a loved one or the end of a relationship can result in intense emotional pain, often described as heartbreak. This experience can lead to feelings of grief, loneliness, and despair.

- Jealousy and Obsession: Negative aspects of love, such as jealousy and obsession, can cause significant distress and disrupt emotional well-being. These emotions highlight the darker side of love and its potential to cause harm.

Reflecting on Key Insights

1. The Biological Basis of Love

- Understanding the role of hormones and neurotransmitters in love provides insights into the physiological mechanisms that drive our emotions and behaviors. Recognizing the influence of oxytocin, dopamine, and other chemicals helps explain the intense feelings associated with love.

2. Psychological Theories of Love

- The exploration of theories such as Sternberg's Triangular Theory of Love and Attachment Theory offers frameworks for understanding the dynamics of love relationships. These theories illuminate the various components and styles of love, enhancing our comprehension of romantic and platonic bonds.

3. The Role of Attachment

- Attachment styles, developed in early childhood, significantly impact adult relationships. Secure, anxious, and avoidant attachment styles shape how individuals form and maintain connections, influencing relationship satisfaction and stability.

4. Personality and Love

- Personality traits influence how we experience and express love. The Big Five personality traits—openness, conscientiousness, extraversion, agreeableness, and neuroticism—affect compatibility, communication, and relationship dynamics. Understanding these traits can improve relationship management.

5. Cultural Variations

- Love is a universal emotion, yet its expression and significance vary across cultures. Examining individualistic versus collectivistic cultures arranged marriages, and other cultural practices reveals diverse perspectives on love, enriching our understanding of its multifaceted nature.

6. Impact on Mental Health

- Healthy, supportive relationships contribute to mental well-being by reducing stress and promoting resilience. Conversely, toxic relationships and unrequited love can lead to mental health issues. Recognizing the impact of love on mental health underscores the importance of fostering positive relationships.

7. Love in the Digital Age

- Technology has transformed how we connect and maintain relationships. Innovations in communication and virtual reality offer new opportunities and challenges for love. Balancing digital interactions with offline engagement is crucial for sustaining healthy relationships.

8. Parental Love

- Parental love is foundational to human development, influencing emotional regulation, social skills, and self-esteem. Parenting styles and the intergenerational transmission of love shape children's psychological growth and future relationships.

The Enduring Mystery of Love

1. Unpredictability and Uniqueness

- Despite advances in understanding love, it remains unpredictable and unique to each individual and relationship.

The subjective experience of love defies complete explanation, contributing to its enduring mystery.

2. Spiritual and Philosophical Dimensions

- Love transcends scientific and psychological explanations, encompassing spiritual and philosophical dimensions. It inspires art, literature, and music, reflecting its profound impact on the human soul and society.

The Power of Love

1. Transformative Potential

- Love has the power to transform individuals and relationships, fostering growth, healing, and resilience. It motivates acts of kindness, compassion, and altruism, enhancing the collective well-being of communities.

2. Universal Connection

- Love connects people across time, space, and cultures. It is a universal language that transcends boundaries, fostering empathy, understanding, and unity. Love's ability to bridge differences underscores its significance in the human experience.

As we conclude our exploration of the psychology of love, it is evident that love is a complex, powerful, and essential part of being human. By understanding the various aspects of love—from its biological basis and psychological theories to cultural variations and technological impacts—we gain valuable insights into our relationships and ourselves.

Love, in all its forms, remains a profound and enduring force that shapes our lives, offering joy, fulfillment, and growth. Embracing the power and complexity of love enriches our journey through life, reminding us of the deep connections that define our humanity.

www.ingramcontent.com/pod-product-compliance
Lightning Source LLC
Chambersburg PA
CBHW071246150726

48001CB00018B/215